INVITATION TO
THE NEW TESTAMENT
EPISTLES IV

This volume continues a series of commentaries on the books of the Bible, specially designed to answer the need for a lively, contemporary guide to the written Word. Here is the best of contemporary biblical scholarship, together with the world-renowned *Jerusalem Bible* text. In addition, there are study questions that will provoke and inspire further discussion.

The Letter to the Hebrews and those ascribed to James, Peter, John, and Jude were written to a developing and growing Church that faced opposition not only from without the circle of believers but also, and perhaps more worrisome, dissension from within. These Letters helped to confirm the believers in their faith and to withstand the onslaughts from their enemies.

Just as the Letters spoke to the first Christians, they speak to today's followers of Christ. The problems the Letters raised and suggested solutions for are still found in today's world, and studying these Epistles can be of help, solace, and inspiration.

Invitation to the New Testament Epistles IV presents these Epistles and their message in a format that can be easily used for individual study, daily meditation, and/or group discussion. It is an indispensable volume for any Christian library.

D1707735

INVITATION TO
THE NEW TESTAMENT
EPISTLES IV

INVITATION TO THE NEW TESTAMENT EPISTLES IV

*A Commentary on Hebrews, James, 1
and 2 Peter, 1, 2 and 3 John and Jude
with Complete Text from The Jerusalem Bible*

FREDERICK W. DANKER

IMAGE BOOKS
A Division of Doubleday & Company, Inc.
Garden City, New York
1980

ISBN: 0-385-14799-6
Library of Congress Catalog Card Number: 79-6743

CONTENTS

ABBREVIATIONS OF THE BOOKS
OF THE BIBLE

Ac	Acts	Lk	Luke
Am	Amos	Lm	Lamentations
Ba	Baruch	Lv	Leviticus
1 Ch	1 Chronicles	1 M	1 Maccabees
2 Ch	2 Chronicles	2 M	2 Maccabees
1 Co	1 Corinthians	Mi	Micah
2 Co	2 Corinthians	Mk	Mark
Col	Colossians	Ml	Malachi
Dn	Daniel	Mt	Matthew
Dt	Deuteronomy	Na	Nahum
Ep	Ephesians	Nb	Numbers
Est	Esther	Ne	Nehemiah
Ex	Exodus	Ob	Obadiah
Ezk	Ezekiel	1 P	1 Peter
Ezr	Ezra	2 P	2 Peter
Ga	Galatians	Ph	Philippians
Gn	Genesis	Phm	Philemon
Hab	Habakkuk	Pr	Proverbs
Heb	Hebrews	Ps	Psalms
Hg	Haggai	Qo	Ecclesiastes
Ho	Hosea	Rm	Romans
Is	Isaiah	Rt	Ruth
Jb	Job	Rv	Revelation
Jdt	Judith	1 S	1 Samuel
Jg	Judges	2 S	2 Samuel
Jl	Joel	Sg	Song of Songs
Jm	James	Si	Ecclesiasticus
Jn	John	Tb	Tobit
1 Jn	1 John	1 Th	1 Thessalonians
2 Jn	2 John	2 Th	2 Thessalonians
3 Jn	3 John	1 Tm	1 Timothy
Jon	Jonah	2 Tm	2 Timothy
Jos	Joshua	Tt	Titus
Jr	Jeremiah	Ws	Wisdom
Jude	Jude	Zc	Zechariah
1 K	1 Kings	Zp	Zephaniah
2 K	2 Kings		

GENERAL INTRODUCTION TO
THE DOUBLEDAY NEW TESTAMENT
COMMENTARY SERIES

Let me introduce this new commentary series on the New Testament by sharing some experiences. In my job as New Testament Book Review Editor for the *Catholic Biblical Quarterly,* scores of books pass through my hands each year. As I evaluate these books and send them out to reviewers, I cannot help but think that so little of this scholarly research will make its way into the hands of the educated lay person.

In talking at biblical institutes and to charismatic and lay study groups, I find an almost unquenchable thirst for the Word of God. People want to learn more; they want to study. But when they ask me to recommend commentaries on the New Testament, I'm stumped. What commentaries can I put into their hands, commentaries that do not have the technical jargon of scholars and that really communicate to the educated laity?

The goal of this popular commentary series is to make the best of contemporary scholarship available to the educated lay person in a highly readable and understandable way. The commentaries avoid footnotes and other scholarly apparatus. They are short and sweet. The authors make their points in a clear way and don't fatigue their readers with unnecessary detail.

Another outstanding feature of this commentary series is that it is based on *The Jerusalem Bible* translation, which is serialized with the commentary. This lively and easily understandable translation has received rave reviews from millions of readers. It is the interstate of translations and avoids the stoplights of local-road translations.

A signal feature of the commentaries on the Gospels is that they explore the way each evangelist used the sayings and deeds of Jesus to meet the needs of his church. The commentators answer the question: How did each evangelist guide, challenge, teach, and console the members of his community with the message of Jesus? The commentators are not interested in the evangelist's message for its own sake, but explain that message with one eye on present application.

This last-mentioned feature goes hand and glove with the innovative feature of appending Study Questions to the explanations of individual passages. By means of these Study Questions the commentator moves from an explanation of the message of the evangelist to a consideration of how this message might apply to believers today.

Each commentator has two highly important qualifications: scholarly expertise and the proven ability to communicate the results of solid scholarship to the people of God.

I am confident that this new commentary series will meet a real need as it helps people to unlock a door to the storehouse of God's Word where they will find food for life.

ROBERT J. KARRIS, O.F.M.
Associate Professor of New Testament Studies,
Catholic Theological Union and
Chicago Cluster of Theological Schools

INVITATION TO
THE NEW TESTAMENT
EPISTLES IV

The Letter to the Hebrews
A Letter Addressed to a Jewish-Christian
Community

INTRODUCTION

The Letter to the Hebrews is one of the most eloquent antidotes to anti-Semitism ever written. It is also a masterpiece of invitation to uncommon faith and life.

So little is known about the circumstances surrounding the production of the document that this Introduction must necessarily be brief.

Hebrews can scarcely be called a letter. It stands rather at the end of a literary evolution in the Greco-Roman world during which informal communication underwent a metamorphosis into a sophisticated essay type that has its counterpart in the Addison-Steele correspondence of British literature.

Examples of the various species can be seen in the New Testament: (a) Philemon and 3 John—brief personal letters; (b) 2 John—brief personal letter, but with a large audience in mind; (c) St. Paul's genuine letters—more formal and lengthier than in (a) and (b), but with numerous personal touches (especially Ga, Rm, 1 and 2 Co); (d) Ephesians—formal, with minimal personal touch; (e) Hebrews—highly formal, with concentration on thematic development.

As for the writer, we must agree with Origen, that prolific Christian scholar of the third century: "Its writer is known to God alone." Numerous candidates have been proposed—among them, Luke, Barnabas,

Apollos, Silas, Clement of Rome—but none has secured a clear majority in the history of scholarship.

Adolf Harnack, a notable historian of dogma, suggested that Prisca (see Rm 16:3; 1 Co 16:19; 2 Tm 4:19), better known by the diminutive Priscilla (see Ac 18:2, 18, 26) might have had a hand in the production of Hebrews. Her husband, Aquila, assisted her in the instruction of Apollos (Ac 18:26).

Harnack's view, like all other proposals, met with negative criticism. But a commentator must choose some pronoun with which to refer to an anonymous author. From a pastoral perspective, I think it would be good for men to experience the feeling that women have in running a constant gantlet of masculine pronouns. Since the Letter to the Hebrews is the only New Testament document that legitimates a choice in pronouns, I have opted for "she" and "her." To simplify reference I will apply to her the name *Auctor,* a Latin term for "author."

From the Contents, which presume broad acquaintance with Old Testament and intertestamental history, it might be assumed that the essay was addressed to Jews. More probably, however, we have an admixture of Jewish and Gentile believers, for whom developing opposition against their Christian experience was proving somewhat traumatic. Auctor therefore alternates in-depth biblical exposition with warning and encouragement.

It is impossible to establish the date of composition with any certainty, but sometime in the last three decades of the first century seems quite probable.

For fuller appreciation of our writer's masterpiece, the user of this commentary might consider reading first the translation in JB and then the commentary, at a single sitting, if possible. Study of shorter portions can then be done with extra profit. Such procedure will also prevent a basic crime against the Scriptures—atomistic study of a few verses here and there.

The following outline is designed to highlight the drift of Auctor's rather complex line of argument. It will be well for you to keep in mind that Auctor thinks constantly in terms of *superiority:* Jesus Christ is *superior* to all beings and persons, other than the Father and the Spirit; his priesthood and his sacrifice for sins are *superior* to any cultic institution; and the hope that is held out to Christians is *superior* to any previous experience in world history.

JESUS, THE SON OF GOD AND HIGH PRIEST FOREVER, IS THE CHRISTIAN'S ANCHOR OF HOPE

1:1–4. Link of Old and New Covenant eras.

I. 1:5–4:16. Jesus is the Appointed Son.
   A. 1:5–3:6a. He outranks the messengers (angels).
   B. 3:6b–4:16. First major exhortation, consisting of *warning* and *encouragement.*

   In this first major division Auctor defines the *person* of the historical Jesus in terms of Old Testament definition of the Son of God. Jesus of Nazareth qualifies as the Son of God-Messiah.

II. 5:1–10:39. Jesus, the Son of God, is our High Priest.
   A. 5:1–10. Jesus as the Son of God actualizes his Sonship through obedience to

the point of death and becomes a
priest after the order of Melchizedek.

5:11–6:20. *Warning* and *encouragement* in
view of this instruction.

B. 7:1–10:18. Jesus fully meets the require-
ments of priesthood and cove-
nant.

10:19–39. *Warning* and *encouragement.*

This second major portion defines more specifically the *activity* of the historical Jesus in
the light of Old Testament ritual. Throughout history God's saving intention found expression. Now through Jesus' sacrifice it finds
expression and ratification once and for all.

III. 11:1–13:25. Jesus links us in *faith* with the *faithful* of the past.

A. 11:1–40. Roll call of Old Testament heroes
and heroines.

B. 12:1–13:25. The New Testament believers.

This section constitutes major exhortation,
with *warning* and *encouragement,* and is the
concluding proof that Jesus introduces a superior covenant.

Hebrews 1:1–4
PREAMBLE

¹ At various times in the past and in various different ways, God spoke to our ancestors ² through the prophets; but ·in our own time, the last days, he has spoken to us through his Son, the Son that he has appointed to inherit everything and through whom he made everything there is. ³ He is the radiant light of God's glory and the perfect copy of his nature, sustaining the universe by his powerful command; and now that he has destroyed the defilement of sin, he has gone to take his place in heaven at the right hand of divine ⁴ Majesty. ·So he is now as far above the angels as the title which he has inherited is higher than their own name.

✠

In a preamble worthy of the best contemporary rhetoric, Auctor presents her basic theme. Symbols that God used in the past find their correspondence in the central reality of the present: The exaltation of the Son of God, who gave himself as the climactic sacrifice for sins.

By emphasizing the Son's involvement in the creation of the world, the writer provides a rationale for understanding the superiority of the Son and of his performance relative to *any* created beings, religious figures, institutions, rites, or ceremonies.

Hebrews 1:5 – 3:6a
UNVEILING OF THE SON OF GOD—
JOSHUA-JESUS

⁵ God has never said to any angel: You are my
Son, today I have become your father; or: I will
⁶ be a father to him and he a son to me. ·Again,
when he brings the First-born into the world, he
says: Let all the angels of God worship him.
⁷ About the angels, he says: He makes his angels
⁸ winds and his servants flames of fire, ·but to his
Son he says: God, your throne shall last for ever
and ever; and: his royal scepter is the scepter of
⁹ virtue; ·virtue you love as much as you hate
wickedness. This is why God, your God, has
anointed you with the oil of gladness, above all
¹⁰ your rivals. ·And again: It is you, Lord, who
laid earth's foundations in the beginning, the
¹¹ heavens are the work of your hands; ·all will
vanish, though you remain, all wear out like a
¹² garment; ·you will roll them up like a cloak, and
like a garment they will be changed. But yourself,
you never change and your years are unending.
¹³ God has never said to any angel: Sit at my right
hand and I will make your enemies a footstool
¹⁴ for you. ·The truth is they are all spirits whose
work is service, sent to help those who will be the
heirs of salvation.

¹ 2 We ought, then, to turn our minds more atten-
tively than before to what we have been
² taught, so that we do not drift away. ·If a promise
that was made through angels proved to be so
true that every infringement and disobedience
³ brought its own proper punishment, ·then we

shall certainly not go unpunished if we neglect
this salvation that is promised to us. The promise
was first announced by the Lord himself, and is
⁴ guaranteed to us by those who heard him; ·God
himself confirmed their witness with signs and
marvels and miracles of all kinds, and by freely
giving the gifts of the Holy Spirit.

⁵   He did not appoint angels to be rulers of the
world to come, and that world is what we are
⁶ talking about. ·Somewhere there is a passage that
shows us this. It runs: What is man that you
should spare a thought for him, the son of man
⁷ that you should care for him? ·For a short
while you made him lower than the angels; you
⁸ crowned him with glory and splendor. ·You have
put him in command of everything. Well then, if
he has put him in command of everything, he
has left nothing which is not under his command.
At present, it is true, we are not able to see that
⁹ everything has been put under his command, ·but
we do see in Jesus one who was for a short while
made lower than the angels and is now crowned
with glory and splendor because he submitted to
death; by God's grace he had to experience death
for all mankind.

¹⁰   As it was his purpose to bring a great many of
his sons into glory, it was appropriate that God,
for whom everything exists and through whom
everything exists, should make perfect, through
suffering, the leader who would take them to
¹¹ their salvation. ·For the one who sanctifies, and
the ones who are sanctified, are of the same stock;
¹² that is why he openly calls them brothers ·in the
text: I shall announce your name to my brothers,
¹³ praise you in full assembly; or the text: ·In him
I hope; or the text: Here I am with the children
whom God has given me.

¹⁴   Since all the children share the same blood and
flesh, he too shared equally in it, so that by his
death he could take away all the power of the
¹⁵ devil, who had power over death, ·and set free
all those who had been held in slavery all their
¹⁶ lives by the fear of death. ·For it was not the

angels that he took to himself; he took to himself

17 descent from Abraham. ·It was essential that he should in this way become completely like his brothers so that he could be a compassionate and trustworthy high priest of God's religion, able

18 to atone for human sins. ·That is, because he has himself been through temptation he is able to help others who are tempted.

1 3 That is why all you who are holy brothers and have had the same heavenly call should turn your minds to Jesus, the apostle and the high

2 priest of our religion. ·He was faithful to the one who appointed him, just like Moses, who stayed

3 faithful in all his house; ·but he has been found to deserve a greater glory than Moses. It is the difference between the honor given to the man

4 that built the house and to the house itself. ·Every house is built by someone, of course; but God

5 built everything that exists. ·It is true that Moses was faithful in the house of God, as a servant, acting as witness to the things which were to be

6 divulged later; ·but Christ was faithful as a son, and as the master in the house. And we are his house, as long as we cling to our hope with the confidence that we glory in.

✠

Hebrews 1:5–14

With the help of two quotations, Psalm 2:7 and 2 Samuel 7:14, Auctor first of all affirms in 1:5 the uniqueness of the Son compared with those who are merely Messengers. (Messenger is the English equivalent of a Greek word that has come down to us in the transliterated form as "angel." "Messenger" more readily incorporates here the nuance conveyed by the writer.) A third quotation (Heb 1:6) is taken from Deuteronomy 32:43 and subordinates the Messengers to the Son. The three quotations together display the relation of the Son to God.

In Hebrews 1:7–9, the fourth (Ps 104:4) and fifth (Ps 45:6–7) quotations contrast the relative functions of the Son and the Messengers, with the addition of important fresh information: The Messengers are *spirits,* at the beck and call of their Master. With this set of quotations Auctor anticipates her exposition of the Son as Messiah and as a genuine member of the human race.

The quotations in 1:10–12 (Ps 102:25–27) affirm the permanence of the Son relative to transient phenomena, thereby anticipating discussion of the relative superiority of the Son over the transitory character of Israel's religious institutions.

Finally, none of the Messengers was ever told that God's enemies would be subject to them (1:13; with a quotation from Ps 110:1). Only the Son has this expectation.

Hebrews 2:1–4

Auctor now builds a bridge to the presentation of Jesus in the succeeding section. Basic to her argument up to this point is the assumption that God's Messengers have tremendous power and authority but are far outranked by the Son. In keeping with exalted views of the deity, some Jewish traditions (reflected in Ga 3:19; Ac 7:53) maintained that God delivered the Law through heavenly Messengers (Heb 2:2). Auctor argues that if their messages were validated by God— through the unusual phenomena witnessed at Sinai (see Heb 12:18–21) and through punishments that followed legal infractions (cf. Ex 32)—the same could be said with even greater confidence of the message of salvation.

Auctor purposely reserves mention of the name of Jesus in 2:3, referring to him instead as *Lord*. Those who personally heard him transmitted the message to others, and God supported their words with phenomenal signs, including gifts of the Holy Spirit (2:3–4; cf. Ac 2; 14:3; Mk 16:20). God's extraordinary beneficence, accompanied by dynamic validation of the message of salvation, contrasts with the mode of validation under Mosaic Law. Rejection of such generosity would, in the social-political atmosphere of the times, be considered an incalculable affront to the Divine Majesty (2:3).

Hebrews 2:5–18

After establishing the transcendent reality of the Son, Auctor is prepared to unveil his historical identity.

Her rhetorical tactic at this point is rather subtle. Again she introduces the Messengers, but this time with humanity as the point of contrast; God's Messengers do not have jurisdiction of the world to come (2:5). According to her interpretation of Psalm 8:4–6, a *human being* who is slightly lower than the Messengers secures control of everything.

The psalmist was of course thinking of the assignment given by God at creation (Gn 1:28), and he uses the term *man* generically. But our writer sees the word *everything* (Heb 2:8–9) as cosmic in its scope. Where is the human candidate who can fill the bill? Only *one*— JOSHUA.

Joshua was a name as common among ancient Jews as George or Henry in the United States. The Greek rendition of the name took shape now universally recognized in its transliterated form as "Jesus." This transliteration was used in Christian discussion to distinguish Joshua of Nazareth from all other Joshuas.

(The King James Version of 1611 retains the rendering "Jesus" for Israel's general in Ac 7:45 and Heb
4:8.)

Auctor's audience would immediately grasp the
point of the association between the latter-day Joshua
(Jesus of Nazareth) and the George Washington of Israel's history. And they would be prepared for the
point made at 4:8 where Auctor completes her word
play on the name Joshua-Jesus.

Auctor now proceeds to unpack the meaning of
2:5–9 and explains the necessary connection between
Jesus' identity and the peculiar circumstances of his
death.

In the Old Testament God's elect people are called
children. For the sake of argument Auctor terms them
sons (2:10). God brings them to glorious salvation
under the leadership of *the Son,* Jesus Christ, who
achieves his goal via suffering. By identifying with humanity at the depths of its frailty he is able to blend
sympathetic understanding and religious identity with
the role of mediator and be of service to all who are
tempted (2:18).

The concluding words of 2:18 point clearly to Auctor's ultimate objective: A high level of moral and ethical performance and total fidelity to God in the face of
obstacles. Proper understanding of Jesus' identity and
function will promote that goal.

By virtue of his being the Son, Jesus outranks the
angels. As the Son he participates in our humanness
but outranks all human beings. Finally, as a member of
Israel, he outranks all Israelites, including Moses and
General Joshua. Quite clearly his leadership is not to
be taken lightly.

Hebrews 3:1–6a

In a rather tightly knit piece of rhetoric Auctor rounds out her argument in 3:1–6a: Jesus was faithful, as Moses was in his "house" (=the people of Israel, 3:2). Being the Son of God, the *Messiah* (3:6; transliterated "Christ" by JB) shared the prerogatives of the Builder himself (3:3–5). Whereas Moses was only a servant *in* the house of which he was a member, the Son has authority *over* his house (not master "*in* the house," as JB has it). Here house means the people of God (3:5–6). The full benefits of salvation therefore await those who are faithful to the end and thereby validate their inclusion in the Messiah's house.

STUDY QUESTIONS: What does Auctor achieve by spending so much time on the discussion of angels? When you come to the Johannine Letters you will note the emphasis on belief that Jesus came in the flesh. Why does the author of Hebrews consider such creedal affirmation so important?

Hebrews 3:6b – 4:16
THE NEW SOCIETY OF THE EXODUS

7 The Holy Spirit says: If only you would listen
8 to him today; ·do not harden your hearts, as happened in the Rebellion, on the Day of Temptation
9 in the wilderness, ·when your ancestors challenged me and tested me, though they had seen
10 what I could do ·for forty years. That was why
I was angry with that generation and said: How
unreliable these people who refuse to grasp my
11 ways! ·And so, in anger, I swore that not one
would reach the place of rest I had for them.
12 Take care, brothers, that there is not in any one
of your community a wicked mind, so unbeliev-
13 ing as to turn away from the living God. ·Every
day, as long as this "today" lasts, keep encouraging one another so that none of you is hardened
14 by the lure of sin, ·because we shall remain co-
heirs with Christ only if we keep a grasp on our
15 first confidence right to the end. ·In this saying:
If only you would listen to him today; do not
harden your hearts, as happened in the Rebellion,
16 those who rebelled after they had listened were
all the people who were brought out of Egypt by
17 Moses. ·And those who made God angry for forty
years were the ones who sinned and whose dead
18 bodies were left lying in the wilderness. ·Those
that he swore would never reach the place of rest
he had for them were those who had been disobe-
19 dient. ·We see, then, that it was because they were
unfaithful that they were not able to reach it.

4 Be careful, then: the promise of reaching the
1 place of rest he had for them still holds good,

and none of you must think that he has come too

2 late for it. ·We received the Good News exactly as they did; but hearing the message did them no good because they did not share the faith of those

3 who listened. ·We, however, who have faith, shall reach a place of rest, as in the text: And so, in anger, I swore that not one would reach the place of rest I had for them. God's work was undoubt-

4 edly all finished at the beginning of the world; ·as one text says, referring to the seventh day: After

5 all his work God rested on the seventh day. ·The text we are considering says: They shall not reach

6 the place of rest I had for them. ·It is established, then, that there would be some people who would reach it, and since those who first heard the Good News failed to reach it through their disobedi-

7 ence, ·God fixed another day when, much later, he said "today" through David in the text already quoted: If only you would listen to him today;

8 do not harden your hearts. ·If Joshua had led them into this place of rest, God would not later

9 on have spoken so much of another day. ·There must still be, therefore, a place of rest reserved

10 for God's people, the seventh-day rest, ·since to reach the place of rest is to rest after your work,

11 as God did after his. ·We must therefore do everything we can to reach this place of rest, or some of you might copy this example of disobedience and be lost.

12   The word of God is something alive and active: it cuts like any double-edged sword but more finely: it can slip through the place where the soul is divided from the spirit, or joints from the marrow; it can judge the secret emotions and thoughts.

13 No created thing can hide from him; everything is uncovered and open to the eyes of the one to whom we must give account of ourselves.

14   Since in Jesus, the Son of God, we have the supreme high priest who has gone through to the highest heaven, we must never let go of the faith

15 that we have professed. ·For it is not as if we had a high priest who was incapable of feeling our weaknesses with us; but we have one who has been tempted in every way that we are, though

16 he is without sin. ·Let us be confident, then, in
approaching the throne of grace, that we shall
have mercy from him and find grace when we are
in need of help.

✠

Hebrews 3:6–19

Faithful expectation (3:6) is the thematic introduction to the closely knit exposition in 3:7–19. To appreciate the force of Auctor's argument, it is necessary
to renew acquaintance with the story of Israel's rebellion, as recorded in Numbers 14. At the very point of
entry into the promised land of Canaan they excluded
themselves by senseless anxiety and retreat toward the
past. Jewish Christians might well ask, "What better
assurance of success do we have? Will the same disaster overtake us?"

In answer to the unexpressed question Auctor makes
the following points: (1) Psalm 95:7–11, cited in Hebrews 3:7–11, indeed issues a stern warning but it describes acts of disobedience in the past and does not
put Israel under a ban throughout history. (2) The
psalmist's word "today" means fresh opportunity.
Faithful confession to the end will make the believers
partners with Israel's Messiah in all the benefits that
come with the promised *rest*.

The word "rest" does not refer to an immobilized
existence on some celestial sundeck. As used by our
author it means relief from the oppressive and limiting
conditions of earthly existence. It is a synonym for *salvation*. To falter at the very threshold of its realization
would be an act of imbecility. Candidates for entry into
the *Guinness Book of World Records* might well think
twice before throwing in the towel an hour short of an-

ticipated achievement of a hundred-day-or-more performance.

Hebrews 4:1–11

A nagging fear that someone might consider God's promises to be no longer valid prompts Auctor to expand on the consolatory theme she had explored in 3:7–19.

Faith is the determining factor as to whether or not one enters into the "place of rest" prepared by God. The people of the Exodus failed to arrive in Canaan—*their* place of rest—because of unbelief. In that respect they are negative models for the present generation (4:2). The fact is that *we,* the latter-day Israel, *are* already on the threshold of the Promised Land (4:3). And the model for that place of rest is the seventh day of creation (4:4–11). Just as Jesus is superior to Moses, so Jesus is superior to Joshua-Jesus (4:8), who led the new generation of Israelites into Canaan.

Along the route of such arguments Auctor endeavored to liberate her community from thinking of God's promises purely in terms of external fortunes, such as continuance in the Land of Palestine and participation in the temple cult. Her theological contribution to the understanding of the Christian community as the New Society of the Exodus is immense. God's people, she stresses, cannot permit external structures and institutions to impede their forward progress.

Hebrews 4:12–16

The words in 4:12–13 appropriately conclude a line of argumentation putting emphasis on the creative power of God. In a sharp bit of word play Auctor explains that the same *word* (4:12) that called the heavens into being is one calling all humanity to *account* (4:13), including especially the Church.

Concerned Christians would naturally ask, "But how can anyone satisfy the Judge of all the earth? You say that we should strive to enter God's rest? We certainly would like to, but you make it sound so difficult."

Sensitive to such anxiety, the writer answers to this effect: The same high priest who shared our frailty of flesh and blood was triumphant over temptation and has already gone on ahead of us into heaven (4:14–15). He provides all the resources we need to keep us firm in our pledge of commitment (4:16).

STUDY QUESTIONS: How does Jesus of Nazareth fit the blueprint of the Son of God? How does Auctor understand the word "salvation"? How is her understanding different from what you hear in the evangelistic query, "Are you saved?"? What would Auctor's own answer be to such a question? What misconceptions about life after death does Auctor endeavor to discourage?

Hebrews 5:1–10
UP FROM DEPRESSION

¹ 5 Every high priest has been taken out of mankind and is appointed to act for men in their relations with God, to offer gifts and sacrifices for ² sins; and so ·he can sympathize with those who are ignorant or uncertain because he too lives in ³ the limitations of weakness. ·That is why he has to make sin offerings for himself as well as for the ⁴ people. ·No one takes this honor on himself, but ⁵ each one is called by God, as Aaron was. ·Nor did Christ give himself the glory of becoming high priest, but he had it from the one who said to him: You are my son, today I have become your ⁶ father, ·and in another text: You are a priest of ⁷ the order of Melchizedek, and for ever. ·During his life on earth, he offered up prayer and entreaty, aloud and in silent tears, to the one who had the power to save him out of death, and he submitted so humbly that his prayer was heard. ⁸ Although he was Son, he learned to obey through ⁹ suffering; ·but having been made perfect, he became for all who obey him the source of eternal ¹⁰ salvation ·and was acclaimed by God with the title of high priest of the order of Melchizedek.

✠

But does Jesus meet all the specifications for a high priest? In a carefully constructed line of argument Auctor offers a strong affirmative answer in which she demonstrates that Messiah-Jesus meets all the important qualifications: divine appointment, humanness, and empathy.

As God's son the Messiah will have an enduring priesthood, not in the line of Aaron but in the manner of God's recognition of Melchizedek (5:6), about whom Auctor promises to tell us more.

High priest that he was, Jesus offered up prayers and supplications to God in the face of certain and ignominious death (5:7). The fact that God, even though Jesus was permitted to fall into the clutches of the enemy, *heard* Jesus' plaintive pleas (5:7) would be especially comforting to the addressees. God is aware of the abysmal depth of depression into which believers may sink in the face of repressive societal structures. "I can't cope any longer!" cries a child of God. But there is no need to feel guilty. A state of depression and a sense of being completely overwhelmed are liabilities of our humanness. They do not turn God off. Indeed, the experience of what seems to be the ultimate in disaster may be the supreme moment of obedience. Such was the case with Jesus.

Sonship necessarily implies obedience (5:8). Philosophically put: Obedience is existential sonship. To effect his sonship as the Messiah, Jesus took the ultimate test—a death that appeared to nullify the very concept of a Heavenly Parent and that seemed to belie God's assurance that the Son would be a priest forever, after the manner of Melchizedek. But Jesus did have his high status validated through the Resurrection (5:9–10). And his obedience to the extent of accepting a death of apparent repudiation opens up life beyond the grave for all who obey him.

That God should determine the destiny of human beings in terms of such obedience is indeed a persua-

sive verdict on the validity of Jesus' credentials as the
Son.

STUDY QUESTIONS: Since Jesus suffered so ignomini-
ously, how can Auctor say that his
prayer was heard? What does her
discussion tell you about your own
prayers?

PROPER DIET

11 On this subject we have many things to say, and they are difficult to explain because you have
12 grown so slow at understanding. ·Really, when you should by this time have become masters, you need someone to teach you all over again the elementary principles of interpreting God's oracles; you have gone back to needing milk and not solid
13 food. ·Truly, anyone who is still living on milk cannot digest the doctrine of righteousness be-
14 cause he is still a baby. ·Solid food is for mature men with minds trained by practice to distinguish between good and bad.

1 6 Let us leave behind us then all the elementary teaching about Christ and concentrate on its completion, without going over the fundamental doctrines again: the turning away from dead ac-
2 tions and toward faith in God; ·the teaching about baptisms and the laying on of hands; the teaching about the resurrection of the dead and eternal
3 judgment. ·This, God willing, is what we propose to do.

4 As for those people who were once brought into the light, and tasted the gift from heaven,
5 and received a share of the Holy Spirit, ·and appreciated the good message of God and the pow-
6 ers of the world to come ·and yet in spite of this have fallen away—it is impossible for them to be renewed a second time. They cannot be repentant if they have willfully crucified the Son of God and
7 openly mocked him. ·A field that has been well watered by frequent rain, and gives the crops that

are wanted by the owners who grew them, is given
8 God's blessing; ·but one that grows brambles and
thistles is abandoned, and practically cursed. It
will end by being burned.

9   But you, my dear people, in spite of what we
have just said, we are sure you are in a better state
10 and on the way to salvation. ·God would not be
so unjust as to forget all you have done, the love
that you have for his name or the services you
11 have done, and are still doing, for the saints. ·Our
one desire is that every one of you should go on
showing the same earnestness to the end, to the
12 perfect fulfillment of our hopes, ·never growing
careless, but imitating those who have the faith
and the perseverance to inherit the promises.

13   When God made the promise to Abraham, he
swore by his own self, since it was impossible for
14 him to swear by anyone greater: ·I will shower
blessings on you and give you many descendants.
15 Because of that, Abraham persevered and saw
16 the promise fulfilled. ·Men, of course, swear an
oath by something greater than themselves, and
between men, confirmation by an oath puts an
17 end to all dispute. ·In the same way, when God
wanted to make the heirs to the promise thor-
oughly realize that his purpose was unalterable,
18 he conveyed this by an oath; ·so that there would
be two unalterable things in which it was impossible for God to be lying, and so that we, now we
have found safety, should have a strong encouragement to take a firm grip on the hope that is
19 held out to us. ·Here we have an anchor for our
soul, as sure as it is firm, and reaching right
20 through beyond the veil ·where Jesus has entered
before us and on our behalf, to become a high
priest of the order of Melchizedek, and for ever.

✠

Hebrews 5:11–14

At first reading it seems surprising that Auctor
should approach her auditors so abrasively as she ap-

pears to do in 5:11–14. But even a superficial appraisal
of her rhetorical style indicates that she rounds out a
major stage in her argument with pointed exhortation
(see 3:7 – 4:13; 10:19–31). Comparatively more surprising is St. Paul's no-holds-barred unvarnished lec-
ture in Romans 2, and without the forgive-my-blunt-
language apology of Hebrews 6:9.

Actually our writer's rhetorical tactics at 5:11–14
are quite harmoniously conceived. Development of the
thesis she has just broached—Jesus, priest after the
manner of Melchizedek—will indeed require close attention (5:11). By suggesting that her hearers may not
be ready for such deep stuff she succeeds in exciting
their curiosity and at the same time she offers reasona-
ble motivation for her warning to any auditors who
might have lapsed into false security.

Hebrews 6:1–12

The warning itself is imbedded in a masterfully executed bit of *paraleipsis* (6:4–8). This rhetorical term is
closely allied to the street expression "throwing dust
into the eyes of the jury." In its most unsophisticated
form an orator like Cicero will say of a Catiline, "I
willingly allow his horrible crime to be buried in silence."

Our author does in fact write subsequently at length
about every theme mentioned in 6:1–2, with the exception of the laying on of hands. She knew that her
addressees would not cry "foul!" "She means them, not
us," would say in response to 6:4–8.

Auctor's slightly apologetic tack in 6:9, coupled
with the pastoral commendation in verse 10, would
further tend to expand her rapport with the audience.
Unfortunately the translation obscures Auctor's neat

packaging of this section. The word rendered "so slow" in 5:11 reappears at 6:12, where it is translated "careless." The point is that the addressees are first called "slow" (specifically of hearing). Near the end of the paragraph (at 6:12) they are assured that their anticipated success as Christians will invalidate the use of the term as a description of their sense of commitment.

Once Auctor's rhetorical tactics are diagnosed, it is comparatively easy to grasp her meaning concerning the apparent impossibility of a second repentance (6:4–8).

Exaggeration is a typical feature of Greco-Roman preaching, and orators were fond of presenting the positive against a darkly hued background. By saying "it is impossible" (6:6) the writer does not aim to close discussion but to emphasize the gravity of failure to keep one's eyes fixed on the ultimate goal. With the phrases "God willing" (=if God permits, 6:3) and *"practically* cursed" (verse 8) Auctor reveals the flexibility in her rhetoric. And the phrase "in spite of what we have just said" (verse 9) indicates that her stern warning is not to be taken as grounds for a verdict concerning the addressees' loyalty to their Lord. Certainly it is not to be restructured into a concrete base for dogmatic theology.

In sum, Auctor has executed a consolatory maneuver. Most of her addressees were conscientious and they would wonder whether, like their Jewish compeers of old, they might lose out on their promised inheritance. By herself refusing to repeat the ABC's of faith—although she in effect did just that by speaking sharply of matters relating to judgment—Auctor assures them that they do not fall into the category of backsliders. Besides, their present performance shows where their values truly lie. All that she desires is their further growth in moving aggressively forward to lay hold of the *promise* (6:12). With the enunciation of this last word Auctor clears the way for her theological bravura piece on the Priesthood of Melchizedek.

Hebrews 6:13–20

To strengthen her word of consolation Auctor focuses on God's own reliability and uses this theme as an opportunity to pick up the main thread that was left hanging at 5:10.

God's beneficent and reliable character finds confirmation in two ways. First of all, as *the* Ruler of the universe, God is committed to bestowal of incalculable bounties (6:13). Abraham is Exhibit A for God's promissory note. And the birth of Isaac, after years of frustration and apparent disappointment of Abraham's expectation, was God's way of guaranteeing the fulfillment of the balance: "I will shower blessings on you and give you many descendants" (6:14; see Gn 22:17).

Actually God's promise should have been sufficient. Yet God makes accommodation to the relatively low trust level of humanity and confirms the promise with an oath (6:16–18).

Auctor's use of the temple cult as a paradigm for understanding Jesus' role is intimately connected with her stress on Melchizedek as the model for understanding Jesus' priesthood. With the word "forever" (6:20) Auctor accents the quality of life expressed in the word "hope" (6:18) and gives herself the opportunity to introduce the peculiar qualifications of Melchizedek as a type of Christ (6:19). The conclusion of chapter 7 includes an echo of the termination of chapter 6 ("forever"), and the intervening verses offer the exposition of what it means to be a priest forever after the order of Melchizedek.

STUDY QUESTIONS: Auctor warns against practical theological illiteracy. How pertinent is her warning to circumstances as you know them? If mere acquisition of deeper knowledge is not Auctor's goal, what is her objective? How does this section cultivate a pride in the job of being a Christian?

Hebrews 7:1–28
JESUS CHRIST WILL NOT BE TERMINATED

¹ 7 You remember that Melchizedek, king of Salem, a priest of God Most High, went to meet Abraham who was on his way back after defeating the kings, and blessed him; ·and also that ² it was to him that Abraham gave a tenth of all that he had. By the interpretation of his name, he is, first, "king of righteousness" and also king of ³ Salem, that is, "king of peace"; ·he has no father, no mother or ancestry, and his life has no beginning or ending; he is like the Son of God. He remains a priest for ever.

⁴ Now think how great this man must have been, if the patriarch Abraham paid him a tenth of ⁵ the treasure he had captured. ·We know that any of the descendants of Levi who are admitted to the priesthood are obliged by the Law to take tithes from the people, and this is taking them from their own brothers although they too are ⁶ descended from Abraham. ·But this man, who was not of the same descent, took his tenth from Abraham, and he gave his blessing to the holder ⁷ of the promises. ·Now it is indisputable that a blessing is given by a superior to an inferior. ⁸ Further, in the one case it is ordinary mortal men who receive the tithes, and in the other, someone ⁹ who is declared to be still alive. ·It could be said that Levi himself, who receives tithes, actually ¹⁰ paid them, in the person of Abraham, ·because he was still in the loins of his ancestor when Melchizedek came to meet him.

¹¹ Now if perfection had been reached through

the levitical priesthood because the Law given to the nation rests on it, why was it still necessary for a new priesthood to arise, one of the same order as Melchizedek not counted as being "of

12 the same order as" Aaron? ·But any change in the priesthood must mean a change in the Law as well.

13 So our Lord, of whom these things were said, belonged to a different tribe, the members of

14 which have never done service at the altar; ·everyone knows he came from Judah, a tribe which Moses did not even mention when dealing with priests.

15 This becomes even more clearly evident when there appears a second Melchizedek, who is a

16 priest ·not by virtue of a law about physical descent, but by the power of an indestructible life.

17 For it was about him that the prophecy was made: You are a priest of the order of Melchize-

18 dek, and for ever. ·The earlier commandment is thus abolished, because it was neither effective nor

19 useful, ·since the Law could not make anyone perfect; but now this commandment is replaced by something better—the hope that brings us nearer to God.

20 What is more, this was not done without the taking of an oath. The others, indeed, were made

21 priests without any oath; ·but he with an oath sworn by the one who declared to him: The Lord has sworn an oath which he will never retract:

22 you are a priest, and for ever. ·And it follows that it is a greater covenant for which Jesus has be-

23 come our guarantee. ·Then there used to be a great number of those other priests, because

24 death put an end to each one of them; ·but this one, because he remains for ever, can never lose

25 his priesthood. ·It follows, then, that his power to save is utterly certain, since he is living for ever to intercede for all who come to God through him.

26 To suit us, the ideal high priest would have to be holy, innocent and uncontaminated, beyond the influence of sinners, and raised up above the

27 heavens; ·one who would not need to offer sacri-

fices every day, as the other high priests do for
their own sins and then for those of the people,
because he has done this once and for all by offer-
28 ing himself. ·The Law appoints high priests who
are men subject to weakness; but the promise on
oath, which came after the Law, appointed the
Son who is made perfect for ever.

✠

Auctor counts on her audience being well warmed
up by now and proceeds with the most esoteric section
of her presentation. Its first part is devoted to an interpretation of the name Melchizedek.

Hebrews 7:1–10

In antiquity people often attached striking significance to names. For example, the change from
Abram to Abraham signaled an entirely new dimension
to the writer of Genesis 17:5. Melchizedek's name
means "my king is righteous," but our writer ignores
the pronominal feature. He is from Salem (related to
the Hebrew greeting *shalom*), a name that means peace
(7:2).

These two themes of righteousness and peace per-
vade Auctor's document. The fact that Genesis says
nothing of Melchizedek's ancestry, place of origin, or
his death provides Auctor with a carefully nuanced argument from silence for the *uninterrupted* continuity of
Melchizedek's priesthood (7:3).

Auctor reinforces this main conclusion by showing
under four points that Melchizedek's priesthood is superior to the Levitical priesthood:

1. Melchizedek received tithes from Abraham.
Priests can exact tithes from fellow Jews. This means

they are superior to their own kin. Yet this is all in the family. But Abraham paid tithes to an outsider. This makes Melchizedek superior to Abraham (7:6).

2. *Melchizedek blessed Abraham.* Abraham had received a unique blessing. Yet Melchizedek received tithes from such an important beneficiary of divine largesse (7:7). Quite evidently Melchizedek pulls rank on Abraham and is certainly superior to Abraham's relatively less important offspring, including the Levites.

3. *Melchizedek enjoys permanent status as priest.* Levitical priests receive their tithes and are subject to death (7:8). Concerning Melchizedek there is no record that he ever died.

4. *Melchizedek received tithes from the Levitical priesthood.* Auctor is quick to capitalize on the strong sense of social solidarity characteristic of the Mediterranean world. The Levites, she argues, were collectively present in the loins of their ancestor when he paid tithes to Melchizedek (7:9–10). In effect they acknowledged Melchizedek's superiority.

Hebrews 7:11-19

We may not think much of Auctor's line of argument, but in her day it would be considered impressive use of established methodology. With the superiority of Melchizedek's priesthood firmly nailed down, Auctor moves her rhetorical artillery against entrenched positions of traditional Mosaic Law. Once that bastion has fallen the rest will be easy.

Her tactical maneuver in 7:11–19 operates along the following lines: The *old* order of priesthood leaves us uncertain about our relationship with God. A constant succession of priests is needed to cope with the problem of sins. The *new*-order priesthood of Jesus enables *one* person to hold the position of priest forever (7:15–19) and extends real assurance of salvation; for, as Auctor shortly will argue, Jesus lives forever in God's presence. His sacrifice for sin lies in the past. The future will fulfill the believers' expectation of salvation.

Hebrews 7:20–25

For the first time in her treatise our author uses the word "covenant" (7:22). Formal legal arrangements were ordinarily guaranteed by oaths. The singular significance of God's oath is its ratification of the factor of permanence in Jesus' priesthood, as contrasted with the long line of successors in the old Levitical system (7:23–24). By virtue of his constant intercessions the believers have ongoing access to God (7:25). Such an arrangement quite evidently declares obsolete the old system of sacrificial rites and ceremonies, and Auctor can scarcely wait to spell this out in detail in chapters 8–10.

By way of transition she reviews again the psalmist's statement concerning the new priesthood after the order of Melchizedek (Ps 110:4). It is important to observe that in these verses (7:26–28) she is not first of all describing the *historical Jesus,* but the *Son* who is addressed in Psalm 110:4 (cited at Heb 7:21). Once having laid down the priestly specifications in the form of a Messianic blueprint, she will triumphantly demonstrate that *Jesus* meets all these qualifications. Of course, as is clear from verse 27, Auctor cannot conceal the fact that she interprets the psalm retroactively.

In contrast to the old order of priests, who were subject to removal by death, God provides for a *Son,* whose person and achievement are to be permanent. The Levitical system required repeated sacrifices for sin. The Son will effect a sacrifice once and for all and will never again be subjected to death. This is what is meant by the phrase "made perfect" (7:28), and the climactic performance is ratified by God's oath. The fact that this oath was made after the Law took effect means that the Law—and the covenant established in connection with it—are no longer in effect. The way is now open for detailed exposition of the superior credentials of the Messiah.

STUDY QUESTIONS: We cannot share all of Auctor's historical interpretation of the Old Testament, but why was it necessary for her, given time and circumstances, to argue as she does? How can we use her insight into the problem of dealing with tradition and be helpful to people who are bewildered by changes in ecclesiastical rites and loss of traditional language and ceremony? Is any change in the Church really as massive as that experienced by Jews in the presence of Christian testimony?

Hebrews 8:1–10:18
ALL SPECIFICATIONS MET

¹ ⁸ The great point of all that we have said is that we have a high priest of exactly this kind. He has his place at the right of the throne of divine ² Majesty in the heavens, ·and he is the minister of the sanctuary and of the true Tent of Meeting ³ which the Lord, and not any man, set up. ·It is the duty of every high priest to offer gifts and sacrifices, and so this one too must have something ⁴ to offer. ·In fact, if he were on earth, he would not be a priest at all, since there are others who ⁵ make the offerings laid down by the Law ·and these only maintain the service of a model or a reflection of the heavenly realities. For Moses, when he had the Tent to build, was warned by God who said: See that you make everything according to the pattern shown you on the mountain.

Christ is the mediator of a greater covenant

⁶ We have seen that he has been given a ministry of a far higher order, and to the same degree it is a better covenant of which he is the mediator, ⁷ founded on better promises. ·If that first covenant had been without a fault, there would have been ⁸ no need for a second one to replace it. ·And in fact God does find fault with them; he says:

See, the days are coming—it is the Lord who speaks—
when I will establish a new covenant
with the House of Israel and the House of Judah,

9 but not a covenant like the one I made with
        their ancestors
   on the day I took them by the hand
   to bring them out of the land of Egypt.
   They abandoned that covenant of mine,
   and so I on my side deserted them. It is the
        Lord who speaks.

10 No, this is the covenant I will make
   with the House of Israel
   when those days arrive—it is the Lord who
        speaks.
   I will put my laws into their minds
   and write them on their hearts.
   Then I will be their God
   and they shall be my people.

11 There will be no further need for neighbor to
        try to teach neighbor,
   or brother to say to brother,
   "Learn to know the Lord."
   No, they will all know me,
   the least no less than the greatest,

12 since I will forgive their iniquities
   and never call their sins to mind.

13 By speaking of a new covenant, he implies that
the first one is already old. Now anything old only
gets more antiquated until in the end it disappears.

1 9 The first covenant also had its laws governing
       worship, and its sanctuary, a sanctuary on this
2 earth. ·There was a tent which comprised two
compartments: the first, in which the lampstand,
the table and the presentation loaves were kept,
3 was called the Holy Place; ·then beyond the second veil, an innermost part which was called the
4 Holy of Holies ·to which belonged the gold altar
of incense, and the ark of the covenant, plated all
over with gold. In this were kept the gold jar con-
taining the manna, Aaron's branch that grew the
5 buds, and the stone tablets of the covenant. ·On
top of it was the throne of mercy, and outspread
over it were the glorious cherubs. This is not the
time to go into greater detail about this.

6   Under these provisions, priests are constantly
going into the outer tent to carry out their acts of

7 worship, ·but the second tent is entered only once a year, and then only by the high priest who must go in by himself and take the blood to offer for 8 his own faults and the people's. ·By this, the Holy Spirit is showing that no one has the right to go into the sanctuary as long as the outer tent re- 9 mains standing; ·it is a symbol for this present time. None of the gifts and sacrifices offered under these regulations can possibly bring any worshiper 10 to perfection in his inner self; ·they are rules about the outward life, connected with foods and drinks and washing at various times, intended to be in force only until it should be time to reform them.

11   But now Christ has come, as the high priest of all the blessings which were to come. He has passed through the greater, the more perfect tent, which is better than the one made by men's hands 12 because it is not of this created order; ·and he has entered the sanctuary once and for all, taking with him not the blood of goats and bull calves, but his own blood, having won an eternal redemp- 13 tion for us. ·The blood of goats and bulls and the ashes of a heifer are sprinkled on those who have incurred defilement and they restore the holiness 14 of their outward lives; ·how much more effectively the blood of Christ, who offered himself as the perfect sacrifice to God through the eternal Spirit, can purify our inner self from dead actions so that we do our service to the living God.

15   He brings a new covenant, as the mediator, only so that the people who were called to an eternal inheritance may actually receive what was promised: his death took place to cancel the 16 sins that infringed the earlier covenant. ·Now wherever a will is in question, the death of the 17 testator must be established; ·indeed, it only be- comes valid with that death, since it is not meant to have any effect while the testator is still alive. 18 That explains why even the earlier covenant needed something to be killed in order to take 19 effect, ·and why, after Moses had announced all the commandments of the Law to the people, he took the calves' blood, the goats' blood and some water, and with these he sprinkled the book itself

and all the people, using scarlet wool and hyssop;
20 saying as he did so: This is the blood of the cove-
21 nant that God has laid down for you. ·After that,
he sprinkled the tent and all the liturgical vessels
22 with blood in the same way. ·In fact, according
to the Law almost everything has to be purified
with blood; and if there is no shedding of blood,
23 there is no remission. ·Obviously, only the copies
of heavenly things can be purified in this way,
and the heavenly things themselves have to be
24 purified by a higher sort of sacrifice than this. ·It
is not as though Christ had entered a man-made
sanctuary which was only modeled on the real
one; but it was heaven itself, so that he could appear in the actual presence of God on our behalf.
25 And he does not have to offer himself again and
again, like the high priest going into the sanctuary
year after year with the blood that is not his own,
26 or else he would have had to suffer over and over
again since the world began. Instead of that, he
has made his appearance once and for all, now
at the end of the last age, to do away with sin by
27 sacrificing himself. ·Since men only die once, and
28 after that comes judgment, ·so Christ, too, offers
himself only once to take the faults of many on
himself, and when he appears a second time, it
will not be to deal with sin but to reward with salvation those who are waiting for him.

1 **10** So, since the Law has no more than a reflection of these realities, and no finished
picture of them, it is quite incapable of bringing
the worshipers to perfection, with the same sac-
2 rifices repeatedly offered year after year. ·Other-
wise, the offering of them would have stopped,
because the worshipers, when they had been puri-
3 fied once, would have no awareness of sins. ·In-
stead of that, the sins are recalled year after year
4 in the sacrifices. ·Bulls' blood and goats' blood
5 are useless for taking away sins, ·and this is what
he said, on coming into the world:

> You who wanted no sacrifice or oblation,
> prepared a body for me.

6   You took no pleasure in holocausts or sacrifices
     for sin;
7   then I said,
     just as I was commanded in the scroll of the
     book,
     "God, here I am! I am coming to obey your
     will."

8 Notice that he says first: You did not want what
the Law lays down as the things to be offered, that
is: the sacrifices, the oblations, the holocausts and
the sacrifices for sin, and you took no pleasure in
9 them; ·and then he says: Here I am! I am coming
to obey your will. He is abolishing the first sort to
10 replace it with the second. ·And this will was for
us to be made holy by the offering of his body
made once and for all by Jesus Christ.
11   All the priests stand at their duties every day,
offering over and over again the same sacrifices
which are quite incapable of taking sins away.
12 He, on the other hand, has offered one single sacrifice for sins, and then taken his place for ever,
13 at the right hand of God, ·where he is now waiting until his enemies are made into a footstool
14 for him. ·By virtue of that one single offering, he
has achieved the eternal perfection of all whom he
15 is sanctifying. ·The Holy Spirit assures us of this;
for he says, first:

16   This is the covenant I will make with them
      when those days arrive;

and the Lord then goes on to say:

      I will put my laws into their hearts
      and write them on their minds.
17   I will never call their sins to mind,
      or their offenses.

18 When all sins have been forgiven, there can be no
more sin offerings.

✠

Hebrews 8:1–6

Had Jesus Christ stayed on the earth he would not
have qualified for the priesthood ascribed to him. Mosaic Law is very strict about the kinds of sacrifices that
are to be made, and Jesus performed none of the traditional rites (8:3–4). But like every high priest in Israel's history he did make a sacrifice—*himself* (8:3).
For his offering to be valid he had to enter into God's
presence (8:1). This he could not do on earth via the
temple. But since the temple cult is really only a model
of the heavenly sanctuary (8:5), he entered the reality
itself, thereby mediating a covenant far superior to the
old Mosaic one. And, argues Auctor in anticipation of
her detailed exposition, it is superior because it is
"founded" (=legislated) on superior promises (8:6).
To use a metaphor alien to our author: Jesus cuts the
red tape of liturgical bureaucracy and deals directly
with God in our behalf.

Hebrews 8:7–13

In support of her "great point" (8:1), Auctor ad-
duces Jeremiah 31:31–34. Three thoughts concerning
the new covenant dominate in this passage: (1) God
relates intimately to people not in terms of conformity
to written laws, but with expectation of changed attitudes and of moral intuition—that is, nothing short of a
revolution in personhood. (2) No one is to have an advantage over the other. Under the Old Covenant superior knowledge of legal precepts by those in power
could lead to oppression of the "least" (8:11). Under
the New Order both the lowly and the mighty form a
community of the forgiven. They are therefore equal in

the presence of God, who demonstrates how power is to be used in the interests of the powerless.

Hebrews 9:1–10

Having recited her text the writer proceeds to preach on it for almost two chapters. She begins with a description of the Tabernacle (Ex 25–30). The fact that it consisted of two parts is fundamental to her argument (9:1–4). The annual sacrifice on the great Day of Atonement took place outside the sanctuary, but the blood was offered to God in the expectation that God would pardon the high priest's sins of ignorance and those of the people (Heb 9:7). Sins committed deliberately were not considered eligible for pardon (see Nb 15:30–31). Obviously, concludes Auctor, the regulations relating to dietary matters, ritual washings, and the like could not permit the liturgist ultimately to say, "Now I can stand with a clean conscience in God's presence." An institution like the Day of Atonement gave the lie to such an idea. The many rites and ceremonies prescribed for the Holy Place could only prepare priests and people for *religious acceptance* by God (9:9–10). What humanity needed was a way whereby the Most Holy Place of all, heaven itself, might become accessible to *any*one. This solution is now to be explored.

Hebrews 9:11–14

To catch the drift of Auctor's argument it is important at the outset to note that for our author the term "Christ" was the Greek equivalent for Messiah, which is the Hebrew term for "Anointed One." Readers of modern translations are advised to think "Messiah" whenever they encounter the term "Christ."

Like an envoy from a petitioning Mediterranean city, Jesus presented himself as the Messiah in the heavenly sanctuary. Nor did he appear empty-handed. He had won "eternal redemption," and the blessings would never cease (9:12). Whereas the Day of Atonement took account of *cultic* DEficiency, the Messiah functions as high priest in the interests of *moral* PROficiency. Under the Old Covenant, service to God was concentrated in the hands of the priests. Under the New Covenant the blood of Christ purifies all of God's people for the recognition of what is right. Empowered for service to the living God, they can stop disintegrating themselves (9:14).

Hebrews 9:15–22

In 9:15–22 the argument turns on a double usage of the Greek word for "covenant." To Christians accustomed to Mosaic terminology it would first of all mean the agreement initiated by God, communicated by Moses, and ratified at Mount Sinai. From the Greco-Roman perspective the term would suggest "last will and testament." Either meaning takes account of the writer's stress on the theme of *death*.

As the superior chief priest of Israel, Jesus, in self-sacrifice, functions cultically and cancels liabilities incurred under the Mosaic Old Covenant. This is the backward thrust of the word "covenant." At the same time, death marks the moment of valid entry into the inheritance of the things that were "promised" (9:15). Auctor will now examine these two facets of Christ's achievement via the death route.

Hebrews 9:23–28

Under the Old Covenant practically nothing could

endure God's gaze in the absence of sacrificial blood. The fact that such sacrifices had to be made over and over again indicates that the problem of humanity's relationship with God had not been resolved. Now at last a sacrifice to end all sacrifices has been made. Christ, himself *the* sacrifice, entered into the sanctuary of heaven, the *real* Holy of Holies. When he appears at the end of the world he will not recleanse from sin but rescue his expectant followers from all the oppressive problems of this present age.

Hebrews 10:1–18

At 9:11 Auctor spoke of the good things (JB renders "blessings") introduced by Christ. Here at 10:1 she observes that these good things were the "realities" anticipated by "the Law." To be clear on the substance of these "realities," one must recall that Auctor is still preaching on the text from Jeremiah 31:31–34. The punch line reads: "I will forgive their iniquities and never call their sin to mind."

Under the Old Covenant Yahweh had a retentive memory for sins, and the high priest had to enter annually the Holy of Holies to help God forget. But now, as the result of Christ's once-and-for-all entry into the Most Holy Place of heaven with the sacrifice of his own body, God has a permanent lapse of memory concerning humanity's past sinfulness.

Practically speaking, this means that the Christian community need not spend its time pondering how to satisfy God on all the details spelled out in the Mosaic legislation. If Christ's sacrifice is once-and-for-all, God does not even remember the legislation.

More importantly, such assurance concerning God's way of dealing with sin carries with it a unique moral motivation. If there is to be no more sacrifice for sin,

Christians dare not act as though the Day of Atonement were still on the calendar. Therefore, instead of treating sin lightly, with the thought that God will have regular periods of atonement for it, believers are exhorted to recognize their commitment to the highest standards of moral awareness and performance. Naturally, our writer's interest in making her case for new-age Christianity ignores the high degree of moral and ethical earnestness exhibited in pre-Christian Jewish circles.

STUDY QUESTIONS: In chapters 8 and 9 Auctor discusses especially Covenant and Sacrifice. What was inadequate about Old Testament ritual, and how does Jesus Christ meet unfulfilled needs? What does Auctor's argumentation say to us as we examine our own approach to ecclesiastical rites and rituals? How much room are we prepared to make for change, and if so, where?

Hebrews 10:19–39
BE A WINNER!

¹⁹ In other words, brothers, through the blood of
²⁰ Jesus we have the right to enter the sanctuary, ·by
a new way which he has opened for us, a living
opening through the curtain, that is to say, his
²¹ body. ·And we have the supreme high priest over
²² all the house of God. ·So as we go in, let us be
sincere in heart and filled with faith, our minds
sprinkled and free from any trace of bad conscience and our bodies washed with pure water.
²³ Let us keep firm in the hope we profess, because
²⁴ the one who made the promise is faithful. ·Let us
be concerned for each other, to stir a response in
²⁵ love and good works. ·Do not stay away from the
meetings of the community, as some do, but encourage each other to go; the more so as you see
the Day drawing near.
²⁶ If, after we have been given knowledge of the
truth, we should deliberately commit any sins,
then there is no longer any sacrifice for them.
²⁷ There will be left only the dread prospect of judg-
ment and of the raging fire that is to burn rebels.
²⁸ Anyone who disregards the Law of Moses is ruth-
lessly put to death on the word of two witnesses
²⁹ or three; ·and you may be sure that anyone who
tramples on the Son of God, and who treats the
blood of the covenant which sanctified him as if
it were not holy, and who insults the Spirit of
grace, will be condemned to a far severer pun-
³⁰ ishment. ·We are all aware who it was that said:
Vengeance is mine; I will repay. And again: The

31 Lord will judge his people. ·It is a dreadful thing
to fall into the hands of the living God.

32   Remember all the sufferings that you had to
meet after you received the light, in earlier days;

33 sometimes by being yourselves publicly exposed
to insults and violence, and sometimes as associates of others who were treated in the same way.

34 For you not only shared in the sufferings of those
who were in prison, but you happily accepted being stripped of your belongings, knowing that you

35 owned something that was better and lasting. ·Be
as confident now, then, since the reward is so

36 great. ·You will need endurance to do God's will
and gain what he has promised.

37   Only a little while now, a very little while,
and the one that is coming will have come; he
will not delay.

38   The righteous man will live by faith,
but if he draws back, my soul will take no
pleasure in him.

39 You and I are not the sort of people who draw
back, and are lost by it; we are the sort who keep
faithful until our souls are saved.

·   ✠

Hebrews 10:19–25

Under the Old Covenant only priests were allowed
to enter the Holy Place, and access to the Holy of
Holies was reserved for the high priest, and for but one
day annually. Under the New Covenant Christ has
eliminated all grounds for anxiety about approaching
God.

Just as the curtain hanging before the Holy of Holies
afforded the only point of entrance to that most sacred
part of the tabernacle, so the flesh of Jesus is the only
route of access to the heavenly sanctuary (10:20).

The curtain of the tabernacle did in fact function primarily as a barrier, but Auctor's point is that the aspect of barrier gives way to one of accessibility. In connection with Jesus, all believers—they make up the "house of God" (10:21)—can have unimpeded audience with the very Head of the Universe.

No propagandist for a poor-worm theology, Auctor stirs her hearers with a vibrant appeal for firm commitment. When Israel was sprinkled with the blood of the bulls, all participants at Sinai agreed to perform everything God had commanded (Ex 24:3-8). In the case of Christians the blood of Jesus has sprinkled their deepest selves, and their baptism with water commits them in mind and body to unadulterated goodness (Heb 10:22). God is reliable, and will bring to completion all that has been promised.

The Christian message does not endorse an egotistical lifestyle nor the purchase of inner serenity at the expense of noninvolvement, fair-weather allegiance, and opportunistic religiosity. Rather, it urges everyone in the community of Christ to acquire a reputation for quality performance, with emphasis on enthusiastic interest in others (10:23-24).

Regular gatherings of the Christians in a given locale offer ideal opportunities for mutual encouragement. Evidently exhortation in the early Church was not left solely in the hands of the presiding elder, minister, or priest; and group therapy is not a twentieth-century development. If some were neglecting the assembly in response to local community pressures or because of disenchantment over the delay of Christ's return, Auctor is quick to remind them that the Day of Judgment is certainly close. Therefore they are to be especially attentive and all the more faithful in discharging their mutual obligations (10:25).

Hebrews 10:26–31

At first reading, 10:26–31 sounds extremely ominous. And it is. But it must be understood from Auctor's perspective of the mindset and circumstances of
her audience.

By stressing the certainty of the climactic judgment,
Auctor offers firm consolation to her audience. They
are on target in their commitment to lofty standards of
fidelity to Jesus Christ. They are on the winning side!
On the other hand, if any in the Church think that God
is soft on sin, Auctor's rhetoric aims to win them to
second thoughts.

In view of the extraordinary mercy displayed in
Jesus Christ's once-for-all sacrifice there must be no
fallback on cultic wheeler-dealing, which Auctor had
earlier termed fresh crucifixion of the Son of God
(6:6). That would be tantamount to the most flagrant
counterrevolutionary activity, for it would be an at-
tempt to reverse the inexorable tide of divinely controlled history.

Hebrews 10:32–39

In her warmest pastoral manner Auctor relieves the
necessary sternness of her rhetoric in 10:26–31 with a
theme of assured success. "In days gone by there were
times, I wager, when you thought you'd never make it.
But you did. And that was when you had far less experience."

Auctor's words about political imprisonment
(10:34) suggest how dangerous Christianity can be
when God's challenge to love and commitment is taken
seriously. The Dietrich Bonhoefers, the Martin Luther
Kings, the John Tietjens, the Gustavo Gutierrezes, and

all who speak with boldness in the face of oppression, whatever forms it may take, are among the more accurate interpreters of our author's words. Auctor leaves room for recognition that some in the community will be more articulate than others, more inclined to operate on the frontiers of interest in justice and basic human rights. Since guilt by association will involve the entire community, the pressure will be strong, even from within the Church, to cool it. Economic reprisals are the feature weapons of power-hungry establishments. In the face of it all, Christians are invited to maintain their identity.

The translation "Be as confident now" (10:35) conceals the fact that this phrase renders the same Greek word translated earlier in 10:19 with "have the right." At 10:35 Auctor in effect says: "Don't give up now your practice of speaking freely." This counsel staggers the imagination. It was given to people under the magistracy of Rome, at a time in which freedom of speech was not a constitutional right.

To be known for endurance in the face of obstacles was one of the most highly prized goals in the author's time. Hold out just a bit longer, Auctor says, and the prize will be yours. The full endowment of the age to come (="until our souls are saved") awaits the courageous performer (10:39). This thematic crescendo gives the author opportunity to express the key word that will run through chapter 11: FAITH.

STUDY QUESTIONS: Sometimes we try to impress God with how badly we feel about some sin and we refuse even to accept forgiveness. What is Auctor's solution to the problem of guilt? In what way might you employ religious

rites as a means to con God? What
resources does Auctor present for
leading a new life? According to
Auctor, what is the point of "going
to church"?

Hebrews 11
ROLL CALL OF THE FAITHFUL

¹ **11** Only faith can guarantee the blessings that we hope for, or prove the existence of the ² realities that at present remain unseen. ·It was for faith that our ancestors were commended.

³ It is by faith that we understand that the world was created by one word from God, so that no apparent cause can account for the things we can see.

⁴ It was because of his faith that Abel offered God a better sacrifice than Cain, and for that he was declared to be righteous when God made acknowledgment of his offerings. Though he is dead, he still speaks by faith.

⁵ It was because of his faith that Enoch was taken up and did not have to experience death: he was not to be found because God had taken him. This was because before his assumption it ⁶ is attested that he had pleased God. ·Now it is impossible to please God without faith, since anyone who comes to him must believe that he exists and rewards those who try to find him.

⁷ It was through his faith that Noah, when he had been warned by God of something that had never been seen before, felt a holy fear and built an ark to save his family. By his faith the world was convicted, and he was able to claim the righteousness which is the reward of faith.

⁸ It was by faith that Abraham obeyed the call to set out for a country that was the inheritance given to him and his descendants, and that he set ⁹ out without knowing where he was going. ·By

faith he arrived, as a foreigner, in the Promised
Land, and lived there as if in a strange country,
with Isaac and Jacob, who were heirs with him
10 of the same promise. ·They lived there in tents
while he looked forward to a city founded, designed and built by God.

11 It was equally by faith that Sarah, in spite of
being past the age, was made able to conceive,
because she believed that he who had made the
12 promise would be faithful to it. ·Because of this,
there came from one man, and one who was
already as good as dead himself, more descendants than could be counted, as many as the stars
of heaven or the grains of sand on the seashore.

13 All these died in faith, before receiving any of
the things that had been promised, but they saw
them in the far distance and welcomed them,
recognizing that they were only strangers and
14 nomads on earth. ·People who use such terms
about themselves make it quite plain that they
15 are in search of their real homeland. ·They can
hardly have meant the country they came from,
since they had the opportunity to go back to it;
16 but in fact they were longing for a better homeland, their heavenly homeland. That is why God is
not ashamed to be called their God, since he has
founded the city for them.

17 It was by faith that Abraham, when put to the
test, offered up Isaac. He offered to sacrifice his
only son even though the promises had been made
18 to him ·and he had been told: It is through Isaac
19 that your name will be carried on. ·He was confident that God had the power even to raise the
dead; and so, figuratively speaking, he was given
back Isaac from the dead.

20 It was by faith that this same Isaac gave his
blessing to Jacob and Esau for the still distant
21 future. ·By faith Jacob, when he was dying,
blessed each of Joseph's sons, leaning on the end
22 of his stick as though bowing to pray. ·It was by
faith that, when he was about to die, Joseph recalled the Exodus of the Israelites and made the
arrangements for his own burial.

23   It was by faith that Moses, when he was born, was hidden by his parents for three months; they defied the royal edict when they saw he was such
24 a fine child. ·It was by faith that, when he grew to manhood, Moses refused to be known as the
25 son of Pharaoh's daughter ·and chose to be ill-treated in company with God's people rather than
26 to enjoy for a time the pleasures of sin. ·He considered that the insults offered to the Anointed were something more precious than all the treasures of Egypt, because he had his eyes fixed on
27 the reward. ·It was by faith that he left Egypt and was not afraid of the king's anger; he held to his purpose like a man who could see the Invisible.
28 It was by faith that he kept the Passover and sprinkled the blood to prevent the Destroyer from
29 touching any of the first-born sons of Israel. ·It was by faith they crossed the Red Sea as easily as dry land, while the Egyptians, trying to do the same, were drowned.

30   It was through faith that the walls of Jericho fell down when the people had been around them
31 for seven days. ·It was by faith that Rahab the prostitute welcomed the spies and so was not killed with the unbelievers.

32   Is there any need to say more? There is not time for me to give an account of Gideon, Barak, Samson, Jephthah, or of David, Samuel and the
33 prophets. ·These were men who through faith conquered kingdoms, did what is right and earned the promises. They could keep a lion's mouth
34 shut, ·put out blazing fires and emerge unscathed from battle. They were weak people who were given strength, to be brave in war and drive back
35 foreign invaders. ·Some came back to their wives from the dead, by resurrection; and others submitted to torture, refusing release so that they
36 would rise again to a better life. ·Some had to bear being pilloried and flogged, or even chained up in
37 prison. ·They were stoned, or sawn in half, or beheaded; they were homeless, and dressed in the skins of sheep and goats; they were penniless
38 and were given nothing but ill-treatment. ·They

were too good for the world and they went out to
live in deserts and mountains and in caves and
[39] ravines. ·These are all heroes of faith, but they did
[40] not receive what was promised, ·since God had
made provision for us to have something better,
and they were not to reach perfection except with
us.

✠

Chapter 11 echoes Ecclesiasticus 40–50, but stands
on its own as a monument of prose that ranks with the
best in any language. As an integral part of Auctor's
sophisticated line of argumentation it marks the climax
of her theme of superior advantage enjoyed by Christians under the New Covenant and at the same time
affords a takeoff point for the concluding exhortation
in chapters 12–13.

Hebrews 11:1–3

Faith is defined as commitment in view of extraordinary expectations. It is acceptance of responsibility to
demonstrate that there are unseen realities that have
priority over immediate satisfaction (11:1). Israel's
history is filled with people who developed reputations
for such faith (11:2), which is a vital feature of a theological understanding of creation. Things come into
being after God says the word. Similarly, fulfillment
will follow the divine word of promise, and faith is the
certainty that such will indeed be the case (11:3).

Hebrews 11:4–7

Nothing is said in Genesis 4:3–10 of Abel's faith,
nor are we told why God considered his sacrifice supe-

rior to that of Cain's. But Abel was a good man. And, as Hebrews 10:38 stated, good men live out of faith.

The same applies to Enoch, of whom most later versions of Genesis 5:24 say simply that he "walked with God." But a translation known to our author states in addition that he "pleased God" (11:5). Enoch's experience gives Auctor opportunity to remind her public that belief in God's existence is meaningful only in the context of belief in the rectitude of God's character.

Considered a lunatic by his contemporaries, Noah took on the entire world. On the surface, all odds seemed to be against him, but he had confidence—of the kind Auctor expects of her hearers—that the future would endorse his decision (11:7).

Abel, Enoch, and Noah—all three of the pre-Abrahamic-covenant people—are primary exhibitors of the intimate relationship between faith and performance. After their introduction Auctor is ready to announce the most revered name in Jewish history: ABRAHAM.

Hebrews 11:8–22

Abraham is of special interest because of his insight into divine promise as a two-phase affair. Without hesitation he responded to instructions and left his homeland. Not until he actually arrived in Canaan was he told, "This is the place." (See Gn 12:1–5). According to Genesis 17:5 God promised it to Abraham and his descendants. This was phase one (Heb 11:8–9).

Abraham's actions nevertheless suggested that he was looking to fulfillment of a larger promise. By living in tents, as did also his son Isaac and his grandson Jacob, he showed that he was anticipating life in a city, which the Christian community knows as the heavenly Jerusalem. This was phase two (11:10).

In some embroidering of the biblical record Auctor shows that Abraham's wife, Sarah, was confident that despite her age—ninety according to Genesis 17:17—she would be the instrument of fulfillment for the promise of an heir. Abraham himself had reached a hundred (see Gn 17:17; Rm 4:19). This fact made Sarah's faith all the more spectacular (Heb 11:11–12).

The plural "things that had been promised" (11:13) contrasts with the singular at verse 9, where the term is applied to Canaan as the "Promised Land." So generous is God with surprises that believers can be confident there will always be more than they see at a given moment. The patriarchs, with their eyes on the future, certainly serve as models for the Christian community, which has even greater reason to remain steadfast in faith and hope.

All God's promises hung on the fortunes of Isaac. When Abraham received the order to sacrifice Isaac (11:17; see Gn 22), Abraham was caught between a lion and a sandstorm. If he obeyed the voice and sacrificed his son, the promise would be stifled, for Isaac alone was to be his legitimate heir. If he disobeyed the voice, his relationship with God would be fractured. Dismayed by apparent contradiction in the divine plan, Abraham rose in faith above the peril: "The problem is God's, not mine." Genesis 22:11–14 records that God was satisfied with Abraham's readiness to make the sacrifice and substituted a ram for Isaac.

Isaac shared Abraham's faith and followed an unorthodox procedure on his deathbed. Instead of making Esau, his firstborn, the head of his family, Isaac gave the patriarchal blessing to Jacob (see Gn 27). Auctor infers from this that Isaac put the unseen things of the future ahead of the demands of custom (11:20).

Auctor burdens 11:21 with heavy freight. Her hearers would be expected to know the incident re-

corded in Genesis 48:13–22. They would readily grasp
the point that when Jacob blessed Joseph's two sons—
Manasseh (his firstborn) and Ephraim—Jacob broke
with tradition and gave the main blessing to Ephraim.
Ephraim would be remembered as a powerful tribe in
Israel. Auctor appears to view Jacob as a pilgrim jour-
neying toward the ultimate place of promise.

Hebrews 11:23–29

In rapid movement toward her rhetorical climax the
author introduces Moses, whose story is told in Exodus
2. His parents' actions provide a model for civil disobedience. On reaching manhood Moses refused to play
status-seeking games, for his eyes were on far more
significant recognition. By identifying with God's
oppressed people he was in fact identifying ultimately
with the Messiah himself and became a model for a
later generation (see Heb 11:26). Although Pharaoh
had intimidated him once (Ex 2:15), Moses held firm
in the crunch moment. He had developed the futuristic
20-20 vision described by Auctor at the beginning of
chapter 11.

It took faith to go through with the Passover rite
(11:28–29; see Ex 12:21–30). Would every firstborn
Egyptian actually die? And would the avenging Messenger really spare the home of the Israelites?

At the crossing of the Reed Sea (=Red Sea) Moses'
upraised staff signaled the time for passage (Ex
14:21). When he lowered his staff the Egyptian army
drowned (Ex 14:27).

Hebrews 11:30–31

Who would have thought that the mighty walls of
Jericho would collapse simply because of a sevenfold

processional circuit with a climactic trumpet blast? (11:30; see Jos 6:12–21).

The mention of Jericho provides the rhetorical leverage necessary to introduce the most unexpected heroine of all—Rahab, the traitorous whore. Her story is told in Joshua 2 and 6. She, who had lived in a manner that defied accepted standards of fidelity, made a decision that crystallized her identity as the most faithful person in Jericho. Convinced that God would give Israel the victory, she disobeyed her king and hid Joshua's spies. In return they agreed to ensure her safety. By introducing her in this climactic fashion Auctor in effect says to the guilt-laden and to the fainthearted: If she could make it, so can you. Only repent and believe!

Hebrews 11:32–39

Through another effective use of the rhetorical device known as paraleipsis (see comment on 6:4–8) our author evokes in 11:32 the kind of response generated among sports enthusiasts by a roll call of baseball's Hall of Fame.

Gideon and a hundred cohorts scattered a Midianite army with some of the most bizarre tactics known to military history (Jg 7).

With Deborah as his colleague, Barak charged down Mount Tabor with ten thousand men, routed nine hundred iron-plated chariots, and put Sisera's entire army to the sword (Jg 4–5).

Samson irritated the Philistines constantly with his fantastic pranks. At his death he brought down the house on more than three thousand enemies (see Jg 13–16).

Jephthah the Gileadite tried to secure an armistice from the Ammonites. They declined. He lectured them about the military disaster that befell the Amorites who had opposed Israel on her march to Canaan. They refused to pay attention. So Jephthah chastized them with a humiliating defeat (Jg 11).

Those four names would be especially meaningful because they stirred up memories of the conquest of the land of Canaan. The further recitation of David's name would remind the hearers of Jerusalem and the development of the monarchy. Samuel would be representative of the prophetic ministry in Israel. Together with the other four they provide the background for the performance record cited practically nonstop in verses 33–38. Readers and commentators are obliged to fill in the details, and this can be done with a fair degree of accuracy.

David emulated the exploits of the four judges by conquering the Philistines. All of them "did what is right" as decision-makers in Israel. Some of the promises, such as possession of Canaan, were progressively realized in their lifetimes.

According to 1 Samuel 17:34f., David would kill unreasonable lions. Samson tore one apart (Jg 14:5–6) as though it were a kid. And Daniel simply muzzled them (Dn 6:22). Shadrach, Meshech, and Abednego seemed to be made of asbestos (Dn 3:24). Some, like David (1 S 18:11; 19:10) and Elijah (1 K 19:10), had narrow escapes at the point of a weapon. Unbearded David toppled the giant Goliath (1 S 17). From the beginning of Israel's history down to the times of the Maccabees (see 1 M 3 and 4), Israel's heroes periodically humbled her various enemies. So much and more Hebrews 11:34 leaves to the imagination.

Even death succumbed to prophetic power, reports 11:35. At Sarepta Elijah raised a widow's son (1 K 17:22). And Elisha, in a posture akin to mouth-to-

mouth resuscitation, restored the Shunnamite's son to
life (2 K 4:34).

Auctor's suggestion of stories like these casts a ray
of light and hope over the succeeding description in
which she turns from successful exploits to the ma-
cabre price that was sometimes paid for commitment to
Yahweh.

The experiences recounted in 11:36–37 are among
the ultimate in expression of faithful endurance. Auditors of the epistle might well think of Eleazar the
scribe, who submitted to torture rather than eat pork
(2 M 6:19). Prophets like Micaiah (1 K 22:24) and
Jeremiah (Jr 20:2) were mocked. Seven brothers refused to eat pork and were flogged (2 M 7:1). Jeremiah did time in chains (Jr 40:1). Zechariah, son of
Jehoiada the priest, was stoned (2 Ch 24:21). According to nonbiblical tradition, Isaiah was sawn in two
under King Manasseh. Others, including Elijah's col-
leagues, died under the sword (1 K 19:10). King Je-
hoiakim dispatched the prophet Uriah in similar fashion (Jr 26:23).

Far from being in retreat from the world, they were
front-line activists. They were frequently viewed as
offbeat, flaky, eccentric, and uninformed about political, economic, and religious realities. Refusing to sacrifice freedom of speech for endorsement of corrupt
political, economic, and religious establishments, they
continued to speak words of power to power. Reprisal
came swiftly. Elijah and Elisha, to cite but two, were
forced to spend their time far from the customary
haunts of people and sometimes at an extreme poverty
level (see 1 K 17:6; 19:13). In passing such verdicts
the world pronounced judgment on itself (Heb 11:38).

Since none of the addressees had probably been exposed to anything approximating the horrors just cited,
the author could count on them being somewhat sheep-

ish about registering complaints concerning their relatively petty tribulations. The heroes of old held out for a promise they never saw fulfilled. Christians, on the other hand, enjoy the present assurance of the long-awaited Messiah, who at the very moment intercedes for them in God's presence. Reinforcement of the moral and ethical implications of such privilege is now the author's concluding objective.

STUDY QUESTIONS: How does chapter 11 tie in with the rest of Auctor's presentation? What anti-Semitic points of view that occasionally surface in conversation among Christians are discouraged by the argumentation in chapter 11? First-century Christians did not live in the kind of open society we enjoy. As you ponder your own constitutional advantages, what would you have to do and say in the line of justice in order to undergo even a fraction of the experiences cited in chapter 11?

SO CLOSE! DON'T FALTER NOW!

¹ 12 With so many witnesses in a great cloud on every side of us, we too, then, should throw off everything that hinders us, especially the sin that clings so easily, and keep running steadily in ² the race we have started. ·Let us not lose sight of Jesus, who leads us in our faith and brings it to perfection: for the sake of the joy which was still in the future, he endured the cross, disregarding the shamefulness of it, and from now on has taken his place at the right of God's throne. ³ Think of the way he stood such opposition from sinners and then you will not give up for want of ⁴ courage. ·In the fight against sin, you have not yet had to keep fighting to the point of death.

⁵ Have you forgotten that encouraging text in which you are addressed as sons? My son, when the Lord corrects you, do not treat it lightly; but do not get discouraged when he reprimands you. ⁶ For the Lord trains the ones that he loves and he punishes all those that he acknowledges as his ⁷ sons. ·Suffering is part of your training; God is treating you as his sons. Has there ever been any ⁸ son whose father did not train him? ·If you were not getting this training, as all of you are, then ⁹ you would not be sons but bastards. ·Besides, we have all had our human fathers who punished us, and we respected them for it; we ought to be even more willing to submit ourselves to our spiritual ¹⁰ Father, to be given life. ·Our human fathers were thinking of this short life when they punished us, and could only do what they thought best; but he does it all for our own good, so that we may share

¹¹ his own holiness. ·Of course, any punishment is most painful at the time, and far from pleasant; but later, in those on whom it has been used, it
¹² bears fruit in peace and goodness. ·So hold up your limp arms and steady your trembling knees
¹³ and smooth out the path you tread; then the injured limb will not be wrenched, it will grow strong again.

¹⁴ Always be wanting peace with all people, and the holiness without which no one can ever see
¹⁵ the Lord. ·Be careful that no one is deprived of the grace of God and that no root of bitterness should begin to grow and make trouble; this can
¹⁶ poison a whole community. ·And be careful that there is no immorality, or that any of you does not degrade religion like Esau, who sold his birth-
¹⁷ right for one single meal. ·As you know, when he wanted to obtain the blessing afterward, he was rejected and, though he pleaded for it with tears, he was unable to elicit a change of heart.

¹⁸ What you have come to is nothing known to the senses: not a blazing fire, or a gloom turning
¹⁹ to total darkness, or a storm; ·or trumpeting thunder or the great voice speaking which made everyone that heard it beg that no more should be
²⁰ said to them. ·They were appalled at the order that was given: If even an animal touches the
²¹ mountain, it must be stoned. ·The whole scene was so terrible that Moses said: I am afraid, and
²² was trembling with fright. ·But what you have come to is Mount Zion and the city of the living God, the heavenly Jerusalem where the millions
²³ of angels have gathered for the festival, ·with the whole Church in which everyone is a "first-born son" and a citizen of heaven. You have come to God himself, the supreme Judge, and been placed with the spirits of the saints who have been made
²⁴ perfect; ·and to Jesus, the mediator who brings a new covenant and a blood for purification which
²⁵ pleads more insistently than Abel's. ·Make sure that you never refuse to listen when he speaks. The people who refused to listen to the warning from a voice on earth could not escape their punishment, and how shall we escape if we turn

away from a voice that warns us from heaven?
26 That time his voice made the earth shake, but
now he has given us this promise: I shall make
the earth shake once more and not only the earth
27 but heaven as well. ·The words once more show
that since the things being shaken are created
things, they are going to be changed, so that the
28 unshakable things will be left. ·We have been
given possession of an unshakable kingdom. Let
us therefore hold on to the grace that we have
been given and use it to worship God in the way
that he finds acceptable, in reverence and fear.
29 For our God is a consuming fire.

✠

The sports stadium is filled to capacity. In the vast
sea of spectators one can glimpse the faces of Abel,
Enoch, David, and all who had already put out their
best. Some of them had paid even with blood for their
faithful witness to God. Now the reputation of the
writer's contemporaries and of all Christians to time's
end is on the line.

Hebrews 12:1–3

In antiquity athletes stripped to the skin for total
freedom of movement. Sin is a drag and must be eliminated, urges Auctor (12:1). Body, mind, and spirit
must conspire together for utmost performance in the
far more important race of life. Roger Bannister, the
great mile runner, is Auctor's most eloquent interpreter: "The aim of the athletic coach should not
merely be to help his pupil to achieve a set performance in his event, to throw the discus 150 feet or to run
a mile in 4 minutes, 10 seconds. It should also be to
show how, through experiencing the stress imposed by

his event, he can understand and master his personality."

Bannister learned his lesson the hard way, in the 1953 Olympic Games. With 11 other runners he walked out in front of 70,000 spectators. Each of the 12 was anxious to be first in the 1,500-meter race. "As I stood at the start," Bannister recalled, "I felt a loyalty to all sports lovers waiting at home. Everyone wished me well, but they could not help me here." Tired out from running in an unanticipated final event, Bannister had trouble sleeping the night before and came in fourth.

A few months later, in December, John Landy of Australia startled the world by running the mile in 4 minutes, 2.1 seconds. Bannister knew that he had to plan quickly if he were to be the first to break the barrier in what the Scandinavians called the "dream mile."

After a series of intensive training sessions he chose Thursday, May 6, 1954, as the day for the ultimate test. With the din of the Oxford crowd in his ears Bannister, paced by Chris Brasher and Chris Chataway, ran the last 50 yards after his body, as he later reported, "had long since exhausted all its energy." He leaped at the tape, he said, "like a man taking his last spring to save himself from the chasm that threatens to engulf him." The announcement came: "Result of 1 mile—time, 3 minutes . . ." The seconds did not matter. They had done it. The three of them! For without Brasher and Chataway to pace him and to elicit the best of his resources Bannister could not have made it. But now, in Bannister's words, "they shared a place where no man had yet ventured—secure for all time, however fast men might run miles in future."

On Saturday, August 7, 1954, enthusiastic crowds filled a stadium in Vancouver, British Columbia. The Empire Games were on and Bannister was scheduled

to race against John Landy, who had earlier lowered
Bannister's record-breaking mark with a 3-minute,
58-second mile on June 21.

Bannister had all he could do to hold Landy at the
220-yard mark. As he entered the final lap Bannister
knew that he was running the whole race to his abso-
lute limit. Then just before the end of the last turn he
hurled himself past Landy. At the same moment Landy
looked over his shoulder. In that instant, recalled Bannister, "I knew that he was unprotected against me and
lost a valuable fraction of a second." Bannister and
Landy together broke the four-minute mile, but Bannister had the edge, with 3 minutes, 58.8 seconds.

"Look ahead," admonishes Auctor. "When the going
seems to be toughest, keep your eyes fixed on the One
who stands at the goal."

After breaking the barrier of the "dream mile," Bannister said: "In the wonderful joy my pain was forgotten and I wanted to prolong those precious moments of
realization. No words could be invented for such supreme happiness, eclipsing all other feelings. I thought
that moment I could never again reach such a climax
of single-mindedness. I felt bewildered and overpow-
ered."

Sensitive to the exultant feeling of the victor as he
received his wreath at one of the many contests held in
the Greco-Roman world, Auctor tells us that Jesus
Christ, in thrilling anticipation of the exaltation that
would be his (12:2–3), endured the most despicable
humiliation—a slave's capital punishment.

Hebrews 12:4–11

Emperor Nero's chaplain, Lucius Seneca, said in his
thirteenth epistle that a true athlete is one who sees his
own blood. In the Fourth Book of Maccabees, a Jewish

work highly respected also by Christians in the first
century, its author proposed the following memorial in-
scription in commemoration of Eleazar the priest and
of a mother and her seven sons, who defied Antiochus
the Great in 167 B.C.:

**HERE LIE THE VICTIMS OF A KING'S
TYRANNICAL RESOLVE**

**TO DESTROY THE HEBREWS' WAY OF
LIFE**

AN AGED PRIEST

A WOMAN FULL OF YEARS

AND

SEVEN SONS SHE BORE

THEY LOOKED TO GOD

**AND ENDURED TORMENTS TO THE
DEATH**

IN VINDICATION OF THEIR ANCESTRY

Then he goes on to say: "The tyrant was their adver-
sary. The universe and living humanity were the spectators. Right won the victory and gave the crown to her
athletes."

Unlike such heroic contestants, and unlike Jesus
Christ, you have not yet entered the main event, exhorts Auctor (12:4). Then, evidently aware that mixed
metaphors are necessary ingredients of creative writing,
she moves from the imagery of the Games to the politics of the home (12:5–7). Proverbs 3:11–12 expressed the sentiment of the ancient world: "Spare the
rod and spoil the child" (see also Pr 23:13 and Si
30:1).

From the reference to "bastards" (12:8) it might be thought that Auctor was insensitive to the problem of children born out of wedlock. She is in fact making her point on the basis of brute circumstance in antiquity. Such children simply did not receive the educational advantage secured by those who were legally recognized. God does not treat us so insensitively, argues Auctor. Precisely because we *are* legitimate children, God educates us, even though the lessons may be painful.

Hebrews 12:12–17

Our author's metaphors are even more energetically mixed in verses 12–13. Weariness generated by participation in the Games appears to be connected with expeditious military routing. Roman roads were marvels of engineering, designed for rapid troop movements. Perhaps Auctor felt that her metaphor of the Games, with focus on the individual, might obscure awareness of liability for community needs.

In Proverbs 4:26, cited at verse 13, the illustration of the straight path is used to sharpen the importance of moral responsibility. The morally weak will have even tougher going if the more experienced and more capable in the Church practice deviousness, cut corners, and engage in the many questionable games that people play.

As Auctor has amply demonstrated, holiness or morally principled living is certain to incur the hostility of less principled people. Accommodation to the *real* world would therefore be a constant temptation, and some Christians would question the advisability of maintaining less popular standards and practices. Others would simply opt for bedding down with the world.

To head off ominous threats to Christian morals, Auctor issues a three-pronged exhortation in support of holiness (12:14–17): (1) To be at odds with Christian objectives is tantamount to apostasy, and Christians are responsible for admonishing those who appear to be excluding themselves from God's grace (12:15). (2) Weakness is excusable, but being a Cassandra is a serious matter. Lowering of morale with a we're-bound-to-lose attitude is completely inconsonant with Christian conviction (12:15). (3) Those who sell out Christian values for temporary personal advantage commit a crime that can be best described as prostitution (12:16).

Esau regretted the fact that he had put his stomach ahead of the blessing he was to receive from his father, and he lost the right to be the ancestor of the Messiah.

In sum, the addressees are not invited to engage in indiscriminate housecleaning but to pass the word to one another that being a Christian means cessation from business as usual. This is the way to seek peace (12:14).

Hebrews 12:18–24

Always the pastor, Auctor moves from a negatively sounding tone to an organswell that celebrates the magnificence of Christian experience. In comparison with it, anything that the world may offer is like the fast-food meal taken by Esau.

The world seemed to come to an end at Mount Sinai, but you were spared all those terror-filled moments, says Auctor (12:18–21). Instead you have experienced under the New Covenant the most unheard-of privileges. In view of that fact, verses 23–24 contain a special appeal. Everyone is called to Christianity as a firstborn VIP. Obviously, then, all need to be on guard against committing Esau's disastrous mistake.

In the face of injustice the hearers are reminded that
their Judge is the God of *all* (12:23). This means that
those who oppose the Christians will one day answer to
the One who is *their* God as well. This Judge has
passed a verdict on all who have already died in faithful commitment: They are innocent of all the charges
leveled against them by the establishments of this
world. Abel's blood cried for vengeance. Jesus' blood
is far superior to Abel's (12:24)—that is, as the as-
cended Lord he not only intercedes for others (this
also Abel could do), but he will be capable of avenging
the blood of his faithful witnesses as well.

Since the blessings are all the greater under the New
Covenant, the responsibilities are also more immense.
At the giving of the Law the earth shook (Ex 19:18;
Ps 68:8). At the end of the New Covenant era all of
the cosmos will be shaken and changed (see Hg 2:6).
Christians have everything to gain or everything to
lose. Far from aiming to frighten her addressees, Auctor wishes to confirm the magnificence that awaits them
(12:28). Whatever you do, don't let your guard down
now! Not when you're so close! The fate of Korah (see
Nb 16) need not overtake *you*.

STUDY QUESTIONS: Toothaches, kidney failure, cancer,
and other illnesses are nonreligious
in origin—that is, they do not ordinarily result from oppressive tactics.
What is the principal source of the
troubles and tribulations envisaged
by Auctor? How does your contemporary experience compare with
what Auctor describes? How might
we Christians actually degrade religion in the sense discussed by
Auctor?

Hebrews 13
FINAL WORDS OF ADVICE

¹ ² **13** Continue to love each other like brothers, and remember always to welcome strangers, for by doing this, some people have enter-
³ tained angels without knowing it. ·Keep in mind those who are in prison, as though you were in prison with them; and those who are being badly
⁴ treated, since you too are in the one body. ·Marriage is to be honored by all, and marriages are to be kept undefiled, because fornicators and
⁵ adulterers will come under God's judgment. ·Put greed out of your lives and be content with whatever you have; God himself has said: I will not
⁶ fail you or desert you, ·and so we can say with confidence: With the Lord to help me, I fear nothing: what can man do to me?
⁷ Remember your leaders, who preached the word of God to you, and as you reflect on the
⁸ outcome of their lives, imitate their faith. ·Jesus Christ is the same today as he was yesterday and
⁹ as he will be for ever. ·Do not let yourselves be led astray by all sorts of strange doctrines: it is better to rely on grace for inner strength than on dietary laws which have done no good to those
¹⁰ who kept them. ·We have our own altar from which those who serve the tabernacle have no
¹¹ right to eat. ·The bodies of the animals whose blood is brought into the sanctuary by the high priest for the atonement of sin are burned outside
¹² the camp, ·and so Jesus too suffered outside the gate to sanctify the people with his own blood.
¹³ Let us go to him, then, outside the camp, and

¹⁴ share his degradation. ·For there is no eternal city
   for us in this life but we look for one in the life to
¹⁵ come. ·Through him, let us offer God an unending
   sacrifice of praise, a verbal sacrifice that is offered
¹⁶ every time we acknowledge his name. ·Keep doing good works and sharing your resources, for
   these are sacrifices that please God.

¹⁷   Obey your leaders and do as they tell you, because they must give an account of the way they
   look after your souls; make this a joy for them to
   do, and not a grief—you yourselves would be the
¹⁸ losers. ·We are sure that our own conscience is
   clear and we are certainly determined to behave
¹⁹ honorably in everything we do; pray for us. ·I
   ask you very particularly to pray that I may come
   back to you all the sooner.

²⁰   I pray that the God of peace, who brought our
   Lord Jesus back from the dead to become the
   great Shepherd of the sheep by the blood that
²¹ sealed an eternal covenant, ·may make you ready
   to do his will in any kind of good action; and turn
   us all into whatever is acceptable to himself
   through Jesus Christ, to whom be glory for ever
   and ever, Amen.

²²   I do ask you, brothers, to take these words of
   advice kindly; that is why I have written to you
   so briefly.

²³   I want you to know that our brother Timothy
   has been set free. If he arrives in time, he will be
²⁴ with me when I see you. ·Greetings to all your
   leaders and to all the saints. The saints of Italy
²⁵ send you greetings. ·Grace be with you all.

☩

In keeping with her rhetorical pattern of sections of
biblical exposition followed by moral exhortation,
Auctor concludes her composition with a major exhortation.

Hebrews 13:1–6

"Brothers" (13:1) comes off more sexist than the original. Unless a text clearly suggests a narrower application, the reader is advised to think "brother and sister" whenever a translation uses the word "brother."

With one part of her brain always tuned in on the Old Testament, Auctor probably thinks of Abraham, who entertained divine messengers before the destruction of Sodom and the surrounding towns (13:2; see Gn 18:1–8; 19:1–3; cf. Tb 5:4–9).

Instead of saying, "I'd rather not get involved," the addressees are to close ranks with those among them who are arrested for alleged subversive activity (13:3). The rendering "in the one body" obscures Auctor's point. To be "in the body," as Auctor phrases it, means to be *vulnerable*. Be sympathetic, you may be next!

In her instruction about marriage Auctor not only celebrates marriage but also demolishes sexist views that put the onus of maintaining the relationship most heavily on the wife (13:4). All sexual practices and double standards that demean personhood in the interests of self-gratification are here put under indictment.

Since sacrifice of principle is frequently linked with anxiety about financial security, Auctor aims to shield her hearers against the temptation by reminding them that the Lord will provide (13:5). Quite evidently the passage is not a platform for maintenance of oppressive economic structures.

The moral integrity of the Christian community is intimately connected with the quality of its leadership. From apostolic perspective leaders are not worth their habits unless they can urge, "Do as I say and also as I

do." And the leaders of the addressees appear to
qualify.

Apparently they were not among the rock-me-no-
boats, make-me-no-waves type of administrators, nor
talkers out of both sides of their mouth, nor sponsors
of a bend-a-little-here-or-a-little-there philosophy, with
a big chunk of reality politics thrown in so as to keep
the volatile effect of Christianity at a minimum. Rather,
their faith, which in Auctor's essay means hazardous
commitment to God in terms of lofty principle and
quality performance, is a model for the entire community (13:7).

Hebrews 13:7-15

So high does the author esteem the leaders that she
follows up their mention with the example of Jesus
Christ. Auctor's description in 13:8 does not aim to
put him into historical formaldehyde. Jesus Christ remains forever the one who is out in front in history, the
one who challenges all systems and activities that demean, degrade, and depreciate human values.

According to Leviticus 16:27, the bodies of animals
sacrificed as a sin offering were burned outside the
boundaries of Israel's camp, and the priests could not
eat the flesh of these animals. In a related manner
Jesus Christ offered himself outside the city to make
his people eligible for participation in God's presence
(13:10-12). Therefore dietary laws and related ordi-
nances are no longer valid. If renunciation of irrelevant
tradition means one runs the risk of being cut off from
customary support systems, that is the price to be paid
for identification with Jesus Christ (13:13).

In the author's time the name of Jesus Christ signaled to non-Christians what the words "communist,"
"liberal," "left-wing," "socialist," and "radical" sug-

gest to many contemporary ears: threat to established order. Traditionalist Jews saw their religious institutions threatened and the delicate stability they were trying to maintain with the Roman Empire jeopardized. Non-Jews would consider their Christian neighbors a threat to their economic and community life, much of which was linked with time-honored religious practices, including private and public festivals at which meat offered to gods would be shared.

Our own social climate is such that in today's world "radical," "communist," and similar terms are ways of saying that so-and-so is not really Christian. In short, what once was the forbidden way is now the accepted way, and the name of Jesus Christ, instead of being linked with what is progressive, creative in ideas, and challenging to oppressive structures, is now interpreted as a brand name spelled STATUS QUO. As a result the Unification Church and the Ku Klux Klan are the beneficiaries of reactions once reserved for Christians.

A free-lance journalist covering a Miss Universe contest said of the winner: "The judges could not have picked a contestant who was farther removed from what's happening today politically and socially. Choosing her was a direct slap in the face of the black Africans and to the girls who had gone out on a limb to protest even mildly the sexist attitudes at the pageant."

The message is clear. The world will penalize anyone who questions its value system. And since religion outdraws even gambling casinos in attracting mountebanks, churches remain a fertile domain for imposters who hawk their quack remedies for the confused and the indecisive, with the stock counsel: When in doubt, play the past.

Hebrews 13:16–19

Since being a Christian was so hazardous, and economic reprisals could be swift, the addressees are urged to place their resources at one another's disposal. Persius, a writer of Emperor Nero's time, said that God is not taken in by material sacrifices, but with the product of an honest heart. Auctor refuses to be outdone by a secular writer and reinforces the sacrificial theology of the New Covenant (13:16).

Anticipating that the leaders of the community will share her enlightened views, Auctor urges her addressees to accept their counsel. Obviously the instructions given in verse 8 still stand. A leader who MISleads is not to be obeyed. To reinforce also a sense of responsibility on the part of officials, Auctor offers two criteria of faithful leadership: (1) Genuine concern for the real well-being of others takes precedence over managerial efficiency. (2) A humble sense of accountability (13:17). Administrators are in turn entitled to joy in the performance of their duties.

Such mutual respect is the antidote to dictatorial power grabs and anarchy. Auctor herself makes no apologies in connection with her prophetic office. She lives openly for all to see, and she loves the addressees (13:18).

Hebrews 13:20–25

Never taking her eyes off the chief administrator of the Church, Auctor makes a last stirring appeal to the authority of Jesus Christ. Through him, not through traditional institutions or secular administrative devices, God equips people to be the benefactors of the world (13:20–21).

Conscious of the fact that some of her essay might have been heavy going, Auctor pleads for understanding. "I had much more to say, but it will have to wait."

Elsewhere in the New Testament Timothy does not come off as a Christian activist, but here he is identified as one who has done time for the Gospel.

Since first-century Christians met in many different houses, there would be numerous leaders to contact in a given area. Auctor did not know about a doctrine of the so-called invisible Church, so she urged her addressees to greet *all* the leaders and all the *saints* (13:24). Between the lines we can hear her say: "If unclear about their qualifications, listen again to my essay!"

Master of her pen until the end, Auctor brilliantly summarizes her main theme through the words "saints" and "grace" (13:24–25). The Old Covenant outlined elaborate provisions to clear (=sanctify) objects, animals, and people for encounter with God. With one spillage of blood Jesus Christ accomplished the feat for all believers. "Saints" are people who have been cleared for entry into God's presence. With the word "grace," all the goodness of God becomes a humanitarian event. Jesus Christ is God's supreme benefaction. Jesus thought the unthinkable, dared the unbearable, and achieved the impossible. As the Presiding Officer in the Church he encourages his people to maintain the style and the quality of life that are uniquely theirs as heirs of the New Covenant.

STUDY QUESTIONS: What help does Auctor give you in dealing with phony revolutionary thinking? How does Auctor's earlier description of Jesus Christ supply the model for leadership among the

Christians? In what ways ought the
Church become more aggressive in
dealing with problems of injustice
and inequity?

The Letter of James

INTRODUCTION

Integrity is a pervading theme in New Testament documents, but no author deals with it in such dramatic fashion as does the writer of the Epistle of James. So concerned is he about high moral and ethical standards that at times one is inclined to think that he regretted the publication of some of St. Paul's thoughts on freedom from law.

On the evolutionary scale of the Greco-Roman letter, the Epistle of James is closer to the essay type of Hebrews than to the more intimate form of 2 and 3 John. This does not mean that the contents fall into clear thematic divisions, but the discussion is not nearly so disjointed as appears to be the case at first reading. To recognize this fact, it is necessary for a Western reader to adapt to organizational features and techniques used by the Near Eastern author. One of these is the device of dialectical opposition.

James' basic theme is God's righteousness, but it is explored from the perspective of an interplay of MORAL STABILITY and CIRCUMSTANTIAL INSTABILITY. Another device is the use of flashback language. For example, at 2:11 the author writes about adultery and murder, yet seems to move on to another subject. Related terminology then appears at 4:1–10.

The essayist's precise identity cannot be determined. He calls himself simply "James," a name as common

in his day as in ours. The view that James "the brother
of the Lord" was perhaps assisted, as JB suggests, "by
a disciple familiar with the hellenistic world and its culture" is not to be lightly dismissed. However, the document did encounter stiff resistance on its way to en-
rollment in the New Testament canon, a strange
circumstance if so illustrious a personage as James the
Lord's brother had written it. It is more likely that a
churchman near the turn of the century would have invoked the name of the Lord's brother, who was once
an eminent leader in Jerusalem, in the hope of com-
municating more effectively in Jewish prophetic vein to
Christians everywhere. Since the Bible in the Sep-
tuagint version was *the* Bible of Gentile Christians, the
writer's use of Old Testament material (as by Paul in
Galatians) would have been anticipated.

Because of the writer's skillful use of diatribe (see
on 2:14–23 and 4:1–12) and reliance on Old Testament agrarian prophetic tradition it is impossible to determine with any degree of precision the specific social
strata of the recipients.

James 1:1
SLAVE WITH CREDENTIALS

¹ **1** From James, servant of God and of the Lord
Jesus Christ. Greetings to the twelve tribes of
the Dispersion.

✠

Israel's exit from Egypt spelled freedom from Pharaoh. From that moment God claimed Jacob's descendants as personal property. Psalmists and prophets cele-
brated the new bondage with words like these:

> The precepts of Yahweh are upright,
> joy for the heart;
> the commandment of Yahweh is clear,
> light for the eyes.   PSALM 19:8

In a vision of the future, Isaiah (65:13) hears God ex-
claiming to Israel: "You shall see my slaves ["servants" in JB] rejoice."

By calling himself God's slave, with Jesus Christ as
the Master, "James" forms a link between his ancestors
and his contemporaries in the Christian community.
The term "Dispersion" recalls the Babylonian Captiv-
ity of the sixth century B.C. It is the writer's way of
identifying the Christian addressees, whether Jews or
Gentiles or both, as God's latter-day Israel.

James 1:2–12
HUMANITY AND THE TIDES OF HISTORY
THE INTEGRITY OF FAITH

² My brothers, you will always have your trials but, when they come, try to treat them as a happy ³ privilege; ·you understand that your faith is only ⁴ put to the test to make you patient, ·but patience too is to have its practical results so that you will become fully developed, complete, with nothing missing.

⁵ If there is any one of you who needs wisdom, he must ask God, who gives to all freely and un- ⁶ grudgingly; it will be given to him. ·But he must ask with faith, and no trace of doubt, because a ⁷ person who has doubts is like the ·waves thrown ⁸ up in the sea when the wind drives. ·That sort of person, in two minds, wavering between going different ways, must not expect that the Lord will give him anything.

⁹ It is right for the poor brother to be proud of ¹⁰ his high rank, ·and the rich one to be thankful that he has been humbled, because riches last no ¹¹ longer than the flowers in the grass; ·the scorching sun comes up, and the grass withers, the flower falls; what looked so beautiful now disappears. It is the same with the rich man: his business goes on; he himself perishes.

¹² Happy the man who stands firm when trials come. He has proved himself, and will win the prize of life, the crown that the Lord has promised to those who love him.

✠

The key word in 1:2–12 and 1:13–18 is "trials," which James uses in two senses. In the first section it refers to disciplinary experience endured by believers, and in the second to moral testing. The Book of Job is eloquent testimony to the intimate connection made by Jews between the two. Although at one point his own wife suggested that he should revile God, Job maintained his integrity to the end.

Our writer's very first counsel (1:2) breathes the spirit of Judith 8:25. In the face of King Holofernes' invasion she exhorted the leaders of Bethulia: "All this being so, let us rather give thanks to the Lord our God who, as he tested our ancestors, is now testing us."

Endurance (rendered "patience" in 1:3–4) was a prized virtue in the Greco-Roman world. Generals and imperial personages boasted of it. James has his eye on the production of Christians who are stable, mature, and well-integrated people. They are to be experts in their profession as Christians. With such rhetoric James demolishes any suggestion of overly timid passivity that the word "Christian" might suggest.

Through his emphasis on "wisdom" (1:5) James lets his addressees know that he is not concerned about developing expertise in worldly affairs but in moral judgment. In order to make sure there is "nothing missing" (1:4) believers should give God an opportunity to improve their moral discernment.

The picture of divine generosity in 1:5 undoubtedly made a profound impression on James' contemporaries. A frequent topic in Greek drama was the instability of fortune. Success had to be tempered with due recognition of jealous deities. As verses 9–11 indicate, James is in harmony with the first of these views but not with the second. God is not threatened by an earthling's success, plays no favorites, and does not give with strings attached.

James' pastoral dimension is not to be lost. In the face of circumstances that might seem to suggest divine aversion, believers are to take heart in God's magnanimity.

Since the ultimate objective is expertise in normal decisiveness, the writer artfully encourages his addressees to present their petitions with firm expectation of results. Waffling in prayer is not conducive to moral triumphs (1:6–8).

Our author's literary strategy becomes even clearer in 1:9–12. His preceding discussion about the need of individual stability derives from his consideration of the vast panorama of unstable fortune. The theme is titanic: HUMANITY AND THE TIDES OF HISTORY.

In keeping with God's character, as described in 1:5, James urges celebration of a shift from low to higher status (1:9). An ungrudging God, not fickle Luck, gives the promotion (cf. Ws 6:1ff.). Similarly, a prosperous person who meets reverses should boast—this is James' one word for "be proud" and "be thankful"—of his newly found debasement, which James describes in words drawn from Psalm 102:4, 11 and Isaiah 40:6–8. Like Job he will praise God for his wisdom and say, "The Lord has given, and the Lord has taken. Blessed be the name of the Lord!" (cf. Jb 1:21). A stable faith in God's goodness is the way to respond to factors of instability in the course of history.

A blessing (1:12) terminates this phase of James' discussion of temptation. The word "happy" translates a term that in antiquity expressed not so much a feeling of euphoria but a judgment as to God's attitude toward a particular human being. Ordinarily the term would be applied to recipients of good fortune. To say it of a person who endured the "slings and arrows of outrageous fortune" would have made a profound impression on Greco-Roman ears.

The promise of a prize and a crown (1:12) echoes bureaucratic rhetoric of the time. God is the supreme philanthropist. Those who love God—that is, put God first in their thinking—are in turn treated as public-spirited citizens who are entitled to appropriate awards for distinguished service. Benefactors in the ancient world were delighted to be feted at a festival during which a wreath of foliage was placed on their heads in recognition of their contributions. The wreath God gives does not perish. It is life itself.

STUDY QUESTIONS: How pertinent to contemporary experience is James' discussion of unstable fortunes? What is Christianity's humanitarian perspective, according to James?

James 1:13-27
A MATTER OF GOOD GENES

13 Never, when you have been tempted, say, "God sent the temptation"; God cannot be tempted to do anything wrong, and he does not 14 tempt anybody. ·Everyone who is tempted is attracted and seduced by his own wrong desire. 15 Then the desire conceives and gives birth to sin, and when sin is fully grown, it too has a child, and the child is death.

16 Make no mistake about this, my dear brothers: 17 it is all that is good, everything that is perfect, which is given us from above; it comes down from the Father of all light; with him there is no such 18 thing as alteration, no shadow of a change. ·By his own choice he made us his children by the message of the truth so that we should be a sort of first fruits of all that he had created.

19 Remember this, my dear brothers: be quick to listen but slow to speak and slow to rouse your 20 temper; ·God's righteousness is never served by 21 man's anger; ·so do away with all the impurities and bad habits that are still left in you—accept and submit to the word which has been planted in you 22 and can save your souls. ·But you must do what the word tells you, and not just listen to it and 23 deceive yourselves. ·To listen to the word and not obey is like looking at your own features in a mir- 24 ror and then, ·after a quick look, going off and 25 immediately forgetting what you looked like. ·But the man who looks steadily at the perfect law of freedom and makes that his habit—not listening and then forgetting, but actively putting it into practice—will be happy in all that he does.

26   Nobody must imagine that he is religious while
      he still goes on deceiving himself and not keeping
      control over his tongue; anyone who does this
27   has the wrong idea of religion. ·Pure, unspoiled
      religion, in the eyes of God our Father is this:
      coming to the help of orphans and widows when
      they need it, and keeping oneself uncontaminated
      by the world.

✠

James 1:13–18

After discussing trials in terms of EXTERNAL circumstances, James applies the same word (now rendered "temptation") to INTERNAL experience. From
his perspective the point is the *shift* that takes place.
As in the preceding discussion, the topic of God's
goodness dominates. No one can say after a wrong
moral choice, "God made me do it." The last thing
God needs, exclaims Jesus ben Sira, is another sinner
(cf. Si 15:12).

The ultimate goal for human beings is perfection or
integrity. This is God's aim for anyone involved in
life's vicissitudes or confronted with the possibility of
shifting from a moral stance to an immoral one. Endurance is required in the face of both external and internal instability.

To overcome moral instability, believers need to
know their point of origin. The genes of desire—that is,
wanting life on one's own terms—carry death. God's
genes determine one's destiny as life. God breeds
believers through the "message of truth," the Gospel
(1:18). In contrast to the fickle appearance of history
and the instability of human character, God remains
unalterable in purpose—to turn believers into show-
pieces of what the cosmos will be (1:18). Such is the

magnificent self-image believers can possess by virtue
of God's generosity.

God is dependable, and there is no need to pay an
astrologer to cast one's horoscope. The heavens may
even display riddles of nonconformity to astronomical
law as we know it (1:17). Yet God remains unchange-
ably determined to bring all cosmic experience to a
fresh plateau of grand design.

James 1:19–27

The key term "message" in 1:18 now serves as pro-
pellant for the discussion in 1:19–27. James' call for
endurance in the first part of his essay prepared the
way for his contrast between the angry person and the
patient listener (1:19–21). Instead of grumbling at
and lamenting life's changing fortunes, believers are to
repent of everything that runs counter to God's ultimate goal (1:12–18). They are to extend a hearty welcome to the implanted word (1:21), the Gospel. Everything else may crumble around them. This word
gives them permanent identity.

At 1:19 James reinforced knowledge with an appeal
for real being. This topic is now amplified in 1:22–25
through juxtaposition of hearing and action. The "perfect law of freedom" (1:25) is yet another term for the
Gospel. It is termed "perfect" because it is *God's* gift
and aims to promote the perfection described in 1:4.
As is the case with one who endures vicissitudes, a person who lives in conformity with the intent of the Gospel can be described as one on whom God smiles
(1:25).

Far from jamming God's docket with unnecessary
complaints (1:26), one ought to take account of the
really enormous tribulations that afflict the lives of
others. Lacking the benefits of Social Security and

other protective legal measures, orphans and widows (1:27) were especially vulnerable to loss of husband and parent. Other people's misfortunes are not neutral phenomena. They engage the moral and material resources of the more fortunate.

"The world" (1:27)—translate "the establishment" —tends to be accepting of misery and even exploits the less fortunate. God's people are not to contaminate themselves with such insensitivity. Vertical consideration of God involves one in horizontal regard for humanity. With this thought James prepares his auditors for the topic of impartiality.

STUDY QUESTIONS: How is the discussion of the word "temptation" related in James' thought to the one on "trials"? The year 2000 will see the world engulfed in problems of incalculable magnitude. What does James say in the face of such a prospect? What are James' terms for the "Gospel," and in what way are they more meaningful than the timeworn term?

James 2:1–26
DO I PUT MY LIFE WHERE
MY MOUTH IS?

1 2 My brothers, do not try to combine faith in Jesus Christ, our glorified Lord, with the mak-
2 ing of distinctions between classes of people. ·Now suppose a man comes into your synagogue, beau-tifully dressed and with a gold ring on, and at the same time a poor man comes in, in shabby clothes,
3 and you take notice of the well-dressed man, and say, "Come this way to the best seats"; then you tell the poor man, "Stand over there" or "You
4 can sit on the floor by my footrest." ·Can't you see that you have used two different standards in your mind, and turned yourselves into judges, and corrupt judges at that?

5 Listen, my dear brothers: it was those who are poor according to the world that God chose, to be rich in faith and to be the heirs to the kingdom
6 which he promised to those who love him. ·In spite of this, you have no respect for anybody who is poor. Isn't it always the rich who are against you? Isn't it always their doing when you are
7 dragged before the court? ·Aren't they the ones who insult the honorable name to which you
8 have been dedicated? ·Well, the right thing to do is to keep the supreme law of scripture: you must
9 love your neighbor as yourself; ·but as soon as you make distinctions between classes of people, you are committing sin, and under condemnation for breaking the Law.
10 You see, if a man keeps the whole of the Law, except for one small point at which he fails, he

¹¹ is still guilty of breaking it all. ·It was the same person who said, "You must not commit adultery" and "you must not kill." Now if you commit murder, you do not have to commit adultery as well
¹² to become a breaker of the Law. ·Talk and behave like people who are going to be judged by the law
¹³ of freedom, ·because there will be judgment without mercy for those who have not been merciful themselves; but the merciful need have no fear of judgment.

Faith and good works

¹⁴ Take the case, my brothers, of someone who has never done a single good act but claims that
¹⁵ he has faith. Will that faith save him? ·If one of the brothers or one of the sisters is in need of
¹⁶ clothes and has not enough food to live on, ·and one of you says to them, "I wish you well; keep yourself warm and eat plenty," without giving them these bare necessities of life, then what good
¹⁷ is that? ·Faith is like that: if good works do not go with it, it is quite dead.
¹⁸ This is the way to talk to people of that kind: "You say you have faith and I have good deeds; I will prove to you that I have faith by showing you my good deeds—now you prove to me that you have faith without any good deeds to show.
¹⁹ You believe in the one God—that is creditable enough, but the demons have the same belief, and
²⁰ they tremble with fear. ·Do realize, you senseless man, that faith without good deeds is useless.
²¹ You surely know that Abraham our father was justified by his deed, because he offered his son
²² Isaac on the altar? ·There you see it: faith and deeds were working together; his faith became
²³ perfect by what he did. ·This is what scripture really means when it says: Abraham put his faith in God, and this was counted as making him justified; and that is why he was called "the friend of God."
²⁴ You see now that it is by doing something good, and not only by believing, that a man is justified.
²⁵ There is another example of the same kind: Ra-

hab the prostitute, justified by her deeds because
she welcomed the messengers and showed them
26 a different way to leave. ·A body dies when it is
separated from the spirit, and in the same way
faith is dead if it is separated from good deeds.

✠

James 2:1–13

James, like Jesus, now blows the whistle on name-
dropping, now-it's-their-turn syndromes, snobbery,
catering to society's exploitative structures, and indul-
gence of accepted neighborhood standards of oppression. To judge from his choice of diction here and
elsewhere in his essay, it appears that James aims to
reach a cross section of Christendom—city and country
dwellers, farmers and tradespeople, with an admixture
of slaves.

Oppressed and exploited people easily fall into the
trap of patronizing and encouraging the very institutions they abhor. One of the religious anomalies of history is the patent classification of congregations, and in
some instances entire Church bodies, along class lines.
Caustically James asks, "Don't you get enough of that
out in the world?" (cf. 2:6–7).

Much of the world's injustice is in fact traceable to
the sin of partiality depicted in 2:1–4; for the definition
of "neighbor" is left to arbitrary choice, and justice
succumbs to private preference. Partiality or respect of
persons prompts citizens to close their eyes to illegal
actions that impose continuing hardship on the poor
and the powerless, who lack the clout of expensive ju-
dicial process or well-financed lobbies.

Since kings have responsibility for all their subjects,
and since the Head of the Universe is the exemplar of

such policy (2:5), Christians are to practice the royal horizontal principle by viewing their neighbors' interests on a level with their own.

The various commandments given by Moses express the Great King's concern for humanity's total life. To rank these commandments in terms of moral preference will not wash, for the One God stands behind all the individual regulations. This is the assumption behind the statement that a sin against one commandment is a sin against the Law in its entirety (2:10).

"The law of freedom" (2:12) is the Gospel. It is the proclamation that God's power is used in behalf of the powerless. Before the heavenly throne no one is exempt from putting in a plea of mercy. It would therefore be the height of folly for anyone in receipt of such mercy to lack compassion for the victims of greed and thirst for power.

James 2:14–23

INTEGRITY OF THE BELIEVER'S PROFESSION OF FAITH has been our author's theme thus far. Self-advertised religious claim is to be accompanied by quality performance levels. Now in 2:14–23 James makes his point as clear as the water of Siberian Lake Baikal. But a word of caution.

One will miss his meaning and lapse into trivial moralizing if James' scenario is taken as a vignette out of actual congregational life. Exaggerated illustration and rapierlike dialogue were typical features of the ancient philosophical-homiletical argumentative form known as *diatribe* (see the Introduction to Jude). The impact of our essayist's illustrations begins to be felt when one realizes that only a sadistic idiot would in real life perpetrate the kind of dialogue presented in 2:16. Pleas-

antries do not fill bellies; similarly faith means nothing
unless it is accomplished by performance (2:17).

James 2:18–26

A series of three illustrations used by a second voice
completes the demolition of the absurd position advanced by the prior imaginary speaker.

No Jew would argue with the proposition that God
is unique. And many non-Jews and non-Christians of
the time would have nodded agreement. But they
would be unprepared for the shocking rebuke: Demons
outdo you. They at least tremble! (cf. 2:19). Now
comes the clincher.

Introduction of Abraham into an argument was a
sure way to win points. Abraham put his life where his
mouth was. He was willing to go all the way with God,
even to the extent of offering up Isaac (2:21). In his
case faith arrived at its *goal* (2:22; the underlying
word, rendered "perfect" by JB, echoes 1:4 and 17).
Also, the Scripture passage that described his relation
to God (Gn 15:6) is seen to be on target. To be called
a "friend of Caesar" was considered the ultimate in
Roman political pull. Similarly, Abraham was an intimate of the Ruler of the Universe. Quite evidently it is
impossible to think of faith as something that can exist
in isolation (2:24).

The final illustration introduces Rahab, Jericho's no-
torious callgirl. This whore is now a VIP in Israel's history. Convinced that Israel's God was up to new things
at Jericho, she went beyond civil disobedience and became a traitor to her own city. Faith is like that, James
teaches. Sometimes it exacts agonizing and ambiguous
decisions. Yet most of the time all that is necessary is
to "love your neighbor as yourself" (see 2:8) with ev-

eryday good manners. With such counsel in mind he
turns to advice on use of the tongue.

STUDY QUESTIONS: It is frequently said that the Church
                  should not get involved in social
                  and political issues. What is James'
                  point of view on the matter? How
                  do you think James and Paul are to
                  be reconciled on the matter of faith
                  and works?

James 3
A GOOD LIFE IS THE BEST TEACHER

3 ¹ Only a few of you, my brothers, should be teachers, bearing in mind that those of us who teach can expect a stricter judgment. ² After all, every one of us does something wrong, over and over again; the only man who could reach perfection would be someone who never said anything wrong—he would be able to ³ control every part of himself. ·Once we put a bit into the horse's mouth, to make it do what we want, we have the whole animal under our con- ⁴ trol. ·Or think of ships: no matter how big they are, even if a gale is driving them, the man at the helm can steer them anywhere he likes by con- ⁵ trolling a tiny rudder. ·So is the tongue only a tiny part of the body, but it can proudly claim that it does great things. Think how small a flame can ⁶ set fire to a huge forest; ·the tongue is a flame like that. Among all the parts of the body, the tongue is a whole wicked world in itself: it infects the whole body; catching fire itself from hell, it sets ⁷ fire to the whole wheel of creation. ·Wild animals and birds, reptiles and fish can all be tamed by ⁸ man, and often are; ·but nobody can tame the tongue—it is a pest that will not keep still, full of ⁹ deadly poison. ·We use it to bless the Lord and Father, but we also use it to curse men who are ¹⁰ made in God's image: ·the blessing and the curse come out of the same mouth. My brothers, this ¹¹ must be wrong—·does any water supply give a flow of fresh water and salt water out of the same ¹² pipe? ·Can a fig tree give you olives, my brothers,

or a vine give figs? No more can sea water give
you fresh water.

13   If there are any wise or learned men among
you, let them show it by their good lives, with
14 humility and wisdom in their actions. ·But if at
heart you have the bitterness of jealousy, or a
self-seeking ambition, never make any claims for
15 yourself or cover up the truth with lies—·principles
of this kind are not the wisdom that comes down
from above: they are only earthly, animal and
16 devilish. ·Wherever you find jealousy and ambition, you find disharmony, and wicked things of
17 every kind being done; ·whereas the wisdom that
comes down from above is essentially something
pure; it also makes for peace, and is kindly and
considerate; it is full of compassion and shows
itself by doing good; nor is there any trace of
18 partiality or hypocrisy in it. ·Peacemakers, when
they work for peace, sow the seeds which will
bear fruit in holiness.

☩

James 3:1–12

James introduces his new topic on the use of the
tongue with the counsel not to run for office of teacher
in the community. Evidently some Christians were
tempted to use the teaching office as an opportunity to
impose their own views and criticisms on the rest of the
family of God.

Adopting once more the style of diatribe, James says
that control of the tongue entitles one to the verdict of
perfection (3:2). On the other hand, the experience of
humanity finds expression in the numerous metaphors
used in 3:3–12, and it may well be that James has
fingered the primary cause of humanity's ills.

The very pessimistic orientation of his diatribe suggests what a formidable assignment Christians have in

connection with a matter that is ordinarily disposed of
as an appendix to moral theology.

Cursing (3:9) is the inveighing of God's judgment
on another person. It is in effect a violation of the admonition expressed in 2:4. What is especially remarkable in James' language is the implicit criticism he
makes of patterns of cursing found in the Old Testament. A directive from Yahweh, like that of Judges
5:23, would be unthinkable for him. (See also Pr
11:26; 24:24; 26:2; Ec 7:21; Si 4:5; 21:27.)

James 3:13–18

Instead of rushing to the teacher's chair, Christians
ought to teach by example. That is the point of the introductory sentence in 3:13–18. Since the position of
teacher also carries with it the possibility of politicizing
the congregation, James warns against divisiveness (cf.
1 Co 1:12).

In an echo of 1:8 James says that instability coexists
with partisan thinking (3:16).

STUDY QUESTIONS: What prompts James to modify Old
Testament views on curses? (See
the OT passages in their contexts.)
How do you distinguish between
partisanship and honest discussion
of varying points of view?

James 4:1–12
HOSTILITIES: PRO AND CON

¹ 4 Where do these wars and battles between
yourselves first start? Isn't it precisely in the
² desires fighting inside your own selves? ·You want
something and you haven't got it; so you are prepared to kill. You have an ambition that you cannot satisfy; so you fight to get your way by force.
Why you don't have what you want is because you
³ don't pray for it; ·when you do pray and don't get
it, it is because you have not prayed properly, you
have prayed for something to indulge your own
desires.

⁴   You are as unfaithful as adulterous wives; don't
you realize that making the world your friend is
making God your enemy? Anyone who chooses
the world for his friend turns himself into God's
⁵ enemy. ·Surely you don't think scripture is wrong
when it says: the spirit which he sent to live in
⁶ us wants us for himself alone? ·But he has been
even more generous to us, as scripture says: God
opposes the proud but he gives generously to the
⁷ humble. ·Give in to God, then; resist the devil, and
⁸ he will run away from you. ·The nearer you go to
God, the nearer he will come to you. Clean your
hands, you sinners, and clear your minds, you
⁹ waverers. ·Look at your wretched condition, and
weep for it in misery; be miserable instead of
¹⁰ laughing, gloomy instead of happy. ·Humble yourselves before the Lord and he will lift you up.

¹¹   Brothers, do not slander one another. Anyone
who slanders a brother, or condemns him, is
speaking against the Law and condemning the

Law. But if you condemn the Law, you have
stopped keeping it and become a judge over it.
12 There is only one lawgiver and he is the only
judge and has the power to acquit or to sentence.
Who are you to give a verdict on your neighbor?

✠

Legislation on murder and adultery came to expression in 2:11. Now James uses these two specifics of the
Mosaic code to sharpen his exploration of problems
generated by partisanship and the rhetoric that accompanies it. And the theme of stability vs. instability continues to thread the whole.

James 4:1–3

The saying about peace in 3:18 affords immediate
access to the discussion on inappropriate and appropriate hostilities. Here again it is important not to
imagine that James' listeners were any worse than a
cross section of members in a church on a given Sun-
day morning. The language is typical of diatribe and
lurid prophetic rhetoric. Similarly, commentators on
the social scene use such terms as "obscene," "ripoff,"
and "rape" to describe entrenched practices of racism,
reckless consumption of vital resources, and other socially acceptable crimes against humanity.

Literalists have difficulty grasping the fact that the
depth structure of iniquity is usually concealed by a
façade of innocuously labeled sin. A few examples
from our contemporary usage should help us understand why prophets like James are forced to sensitize
through provocative diction: Invocation of "the public
interest" contributes a patriotic dimension to established selfishness. . . . "Profit incentive" takes the

bite out of greed. . . . In the interests of "responsibility to our stockholders," corporations can excuse
themselves from involvement in "sociology."

At 1:14 James had observed that misplaced desire is
the seminal cause of sin. The cure, as indicated in
1:16–18, is dependence on divine generosity. Instead
of praying for improved moral performance, we tend,
James warns, to concentrate on material things (4:
2–3). The consequences are disastrous to our human
relationships, James affirms as he couples partisanship
with MURDER in an effort to sound a siren that will
awaken Christians to the perils of party strife.

From scattered comments in the Gospels and Letters
of the New Testament we can see that the use of positions of influence as an opportunity for self-aggran-
dizement was a widespread problem. The Pastoral
Epistles issue repeated warnings against "love of
money" (1 Tm 3:3, 8; 2 Tm 3:2; Tt 1:7). Similarly
Luke 12:41–48 interprets one of Jesus' parables in
terms of its application to the leadership in the Christian community (see *Invitation to Luke,* pp. 160–61).
Rise to ecclesiastical power is invariably accompanied,
as history well documents, by exaggerated insistence on
the correctness of one's own position and the error in
other points of view; by name calling; and by demolition of reputations. Newspapers take their rhetoric right
out of James when they headline ecclesiastical feuding
with such captions as CIVIL WAR or BATTLE
OVER THE BIBLE.

James 4:4–5

The second major crime mentioned in 2:11 was
ADULTERY. James magnifies his rhetorical indigna-
tion by comparing his addressees with adulterous wives
(4:4). From a Jewish perspective God is the husband

of Israel (cf. Is 54:5). When Israel split her time between Yahweh and idols, she was accused of whore-
dom (Ezekiel makes this charge repeatedly). Paul used
marriage metaphors to give positive expression to the
relationship between Christ and believers (Ep 6).

At this point in his essay, James skillfully effects a
juncture with his earlier allusion to Abraham and
Rahab (2:21–26). There Rahab, the whore, was a
model of goodness, and Abraham was God's intimate
friend. Here at 4:4 the absurdity of engaging in hostilities with one another in the name of religion reaches its
climactic exposure in a charge of hostility against God.

James 4:6–12

To engage in the game of one-upmanship is not only
futile, it also is stupid. As was already observed at
1:9–10, God supports the humble and resists the
proud. To elevate oneself by downrating another
makes one a sitting duck for judgment. Self-aggran-
dizement, especially at the expense of another, is
brainless engagement in competition with God and
turns religion into a charade. James had earlier issued
a warning about such double-mindedness (4:8; see
1:8). He had also written about the unity of God
(2:19). Now his hearers can have a still better understanding of what he meant. The lawgiver retains the
privilege of judgment! (4:12)

STUDY QUESTIONS: What other practices or slogans in
your society fall under James' pro-
phetic indictment of murder? Apart
from customary sexual associations,
what are some of the "adulteries"
in which you are tempted to participate in your society?

James 4:13 – 5:6
ARROGANCE IS HAZARDOUS TO YOUR HEALTH

13 Here is the answer for those of you who talk like this: "Today or tomorrow, we are off to this or that town; we are going to spend a year there, 14 trading, and make some money." ·You never know what will happen tomorrow: you are no more than a mist that is here for a little while and 15 then disappears. ·The most you should ever say is: "If it is the Lord's will, we shall still be alive 16 to do this or that." ·But how proud and sure of yourselves you are now! Pride of this kind is al- 17 ways wicked. ·Everyone who knows what is the right thing to do and doesn't do it commits a sin.

5 ¹ Now an answer for the rich. Start crying, weep for the miseries that are coming to you. 2 Your wealth is all rotting, your clothes are all 3 eaten up by moths. ·All your gold and your silver are corroding away, and the same corrosion will be your own sentence, and eat into your body. It was a burning fire that you stored up as your 4 treasure for the last days. ·Laborers mowed your fields, and you cheated them—listen to the wages that you kept back, calling out; realize that the cries of the reapers have reached the ears of the 5 Lord of hosts. ·On earth you have had a life of comfort and luxury; in the time of slaughter you 6 went on eating to your heart's content. ·It was you who condemned the innocent and killed them; they offered you no resistance.

☩

Ever threading the whole is the theme of UNSTA-
BLE FORTUNE, and the section beginning at 4:13 is
James' own commentary on 1:10–11. In the first part,
4:13–17, he moves his auditors to the dramatic infer-
ence that uncritical assumption of self-command over
the future is fundamentally atheistic.

Arrogant assumptions about doing business as usual
are also fundamentally immoral, James explodes in
5:1–6 as he tears injustice to shreds. If faith without
works is dead, misdirected faith will certainly produce
attitudes and actions that are contrary to God's interests in humanity. Oppression and fraudulent commerce
are the necessary end products of arrogant resolve to
bend the world and its resources to individual and cor-
porate self-interest (see Si 13; Is 3:14; Jr 5:27; 6:13;
Ho 12:8; Am 8:5).

The final words of 5:6 are as ominous as they are
poignant. Innocent victims of oppression can offer no
resistance to the system. But, as 4:6 affirmed, *God*
resists the self-sufficient.

STUDY QUESTIONS: How does James 4:13 – 5:6 relate
to what James said earlier? The
United States consumes the resources of poor nations at a devas-
tating rate. What does James say to
us, the participants in this rapacity,
in view of our competitive demands
for services and goods? What are
you, for one, going to do about it?

James 5:7–20
GOD PICKS ON NO ONE

7   Now be patient, brothers, until the Lord's coming. Think of a farmer: how patiently he waits for the precious fruit of the ground until it has had
8 the autumn rains and the spring rains! ·You too have to be patient; do not lose heart, because the
9 Lord's coming will be soon. ·Do not make complaints against one another, brothers, so as not to be brought to judgment yourselves; the Judge is
10 already to be seen waiting at the gates. ·For your example, brothers, in submitting with patience, take the prophets who spoke in the name of the
11 Lord: ·remember it is those who had endurance that we say are the blessed ones. You have heard of the patience of Job, and understood the Lord's purpose, realizing that the Lord is kind and compassionate.
12   Above all, my brothers, do not swear by heaven or by the earth, or use any oaths at all. If you mean "yes," you must say "yes"; if you mean "no," say "no." Otherwise you make yourselves liable to judgment.
13   If any one of you is in trouble, he should pray; if anyone is feeling happy, he should sing a psalm.
14 If one of you is ill, he should send for the elders of the church, and they must anoint him with oil
15 in the name of the Lord and pray over him. ·The prayer of faith will save the sick man and the Lord will raise him up again; and if he has com-
16 mitted any sins, he will be forgiven. ·So confess your sins to one another, and pray for one another, and this will cure you; the heartfelt prayer

17 of a good man works very powerfully. ·Elijah was
a human being like ourselves—he prayed hard for
it not to rain, and no rain fell for three and a half
18 years; ·then he prayed again and the sky gave rain
and the earth gave crops.
19   My brothers, if one of you strays away from the
20 truth, and another brings him back to it, ·he may
be sure that anyone who can bring back a sinner
from the wrong way that he has taken will be saving a soul from death and covering up a great
number of sins.

☩

James 5:7–11

As is frequently the case in our document, James'
language comes at high voltage. Beyond question, as
4:13 – 5:6 attested, he aims to discourage pride and arrogance. Those who thought they might be special targets of his rhetoric might well appreciate his warning
against the sin of arrogance, a fearful crime in the eyes
of religious Greeks and Romans. But his prophetic attack is in large measure designed to offer consolation
to all believers, constituting as they do a minority ele-
ment in the Roman Empire.

A dominant topic in ancient consolatory literature is
the problem of preferential treatment. Job's question is
perennial: "WHY I?" James anticipates similar queries, and he counsels, "Be patient" (5:7). The Lord
will return shortly and will audit all accounts (5:8–9).
So don't complain that someone else deserves to suffer
more than you. Prophets, and especially Job, were
more entitled than you to complaints, yet they are
models of patience (5:10–11). With this admonition
the essayist has almost completed his exposition of the
theme of endurance that was first aired at 1:3.

James 5:12–16

When involved in losses of various kinds, or when suffering an illness, such as alcoholism, one is liable to promise anything to people or to God. "Just one more chance. Please!"

James knows well the broken-vow syndrome and, in keeping with related advice offered by Jesus (Mt 5:34–37), admonishes his readers to confine their promissory rhetoric to two monosyllables (James 5:12). If they still feel the need of emphasis, they have the permission of Jesus to double them (Mt 5:37).

Instead of making extravagant vows, people who suffer a reverse in fortune should pray, and the prosperous should sing a hymn (5:13). In either case God is retained at the center. Similarly James advises sick people to forego impassioned promises in the hope of recovery. Instead they should call on the leaders of the congregation, who will pray for them. From the reference to the "name of the Lord" (5:14) it appears that the writer has in mind exorcism of spirits that were connected with various physical ailments (cf. Mk 9:14–29; Lk 13:16).

From numerous testimonies in the New Testament it is evident that early Christians were exceptionally confident that God would direct power in their behalf in the here and now. Of special interest is the fact that a ceremony of prayer and anointing formed an integral part of congregational experience. Like speech in tongues, the rite of healing, in the form and application known to James, became more and more formalized. In modern times it has made a comeback in the face of developing interest in physical healing through the instrumentality of prayer.

Of primary concern, however, is the perspective that

James gives to the ministry of healing. There is no explicit attribution of healing powers to the elders. Their prayers invoke the beneficent power of God. Second, the entire congregation is involved in the sufferer's problem. Third, traditional assumptions concerning a cause-and-effect relationship between disease and sin are challenged. *If* a person has committed sins (presumably those of which the patient is aware), they will be pardoned (5:15). In other words, suffering of any kind is not necessarily the result of sin, imagined or real. In fact, explains James, *all* Christians, sick or healthy, should confess their sins one to another. The primary sin of spiritual elitism is here struck down with one rhetorical blow, and healing is shown to be available to all. In short, GOD PICKS ON NO ONE (recall chapter 1).

James 5:17–20

With dramatic economy James concludes his essay. At first reading it appears that Elijah is a model for spectacular charismatic performance (5:17–18). But the concluding sentence puts everything into perspective. Far more important than control of the elements is the contribution one can make to another's moral development.

James is aware that everyone undergoes the temptation of assuming that the other is in need of improvement. It comes therefore as a shocker when James writes: "If one of *you* strays away from the truth" (5:19). To stray away from a correct moral decision is far worse than going through a drought of 3½ years. So be thankful when a concerned brother or sister implores the Almighty and admonishes you. Not only will you be saved from the consequences of your present course of action, but also from a multitude of sinful possibilities (5:20).

"Stop your straying" (JB: "make no mistakes"), wrote James at 1:16. Mutual application of the Gospel will call a halt to moral instability, concludes the essayist. It is *the* route to integrity. It is the cure for instability of character and divided personhood. It is the way by which the Giver of all good gifts comes into view.

STUDY QUESTIONS: What is James' contribution to dialogue on "charismatic gifts"? What are his contributions to mental health? What is his contribution to the theology and practice of confession and absolution?

INTRODUCTION

Pastoral exuberance and a cultivated style of expression invite the reader of 1 Peter to explore courageous dimensions of the Christian faith.

As is the case with the other General Epistles (Hebrews, James, 2 Peter, 1–3 John, and Jude), we are unable to establish with certainty the identity of the writer. Most scholars are agreed that a literary connection with the Apostle Peter is at best tenuous. Quite probably a churchman near the end of the first century invoked the name of the great apostle in order to encourage Christians, especially in Asia Minor, to hold their ground in the face of increasing opposition to what non-Christian Gentiles considered a threat to their traditional way of life.

"What would Peter tell us if he were still alive?" The Letter called 1 Peter provides the answers. Like the Letter of James, it falls into the classification of pseudonymous writing, a common procedure in antiquity. Since motive is a primary consideration in determining the moral character of an action, the term pseudonymity is itself morally neutral. In the case of 1 Peter the motive is certainly not to promote false doctrine, nor to create a cultic platform for the writer, but to help the recipients link their present experiences with those of past generations. Actually the writer submerged his own personality so that the apostolic wit-

ness could come through unimpeded. In any court of
law he must be considered innocent of any charge of
wrongdoing.

INTEGRITY IN THE FACE OF OBSTACLES is
the main theme of the Letter. In support of this instruction, Peter (we will refer to the writer by this
name) shows how all Christians, Gentiles as well as
Jews, are in continuity with Israel of the Exodus and
the Exile. Like the Israelites of old they are now in
Dispersion throughout Asia Minor. Through Jesus
Christ God is their Parent. Hence they constitute a
household. Since a household presumes mutual recognition of privileges, obligations, and responsibilities,
Peter offers specific counsel concerning a broad range
of personal relationships.

For much of the insight into Peter's use of the
"house" metaphor I am indebted to John H. Elliott's
thorough *The Elect and the Holy* (Leiden, 1966).

I invite you now to see some of the ways in which
this jewel among the General Epistles refracts the
apostolic light. Especially note the artistic way in
which Peter interweaves moral and ethical counsel.

1 Peter 1:1–2
PRIVILEGED VIP'S

¹ 1 Peter, apostle of Jesus Christ, sends greetings
to all those living among foreigners in the Dispersion of Pontus, Galatia, Cappadocia, Asia and
² Bithynia, who have been chosen, ·by the provident
purpose of God the Father, to be made holy by
the Spirit, obedient to Jesus Christ and sprinkled
with his blood. Grace and peace be with you more
and more.

✠

In one sonorous sentence Peter greets all his addressees as VIP's and signals the major themes of his
letter. Jew or Gentile, it makes no difference. All who
underwrite the constitution of the New Age by identifying with Jesus Christ are participants in a fresh
Exodus and a latter-day deliverance from Babylon.

Like Israel of old the Christian community has in its
own way visited Mount Sinai. There Moses once sprinkled God's people with the blood of bulls and goats. In
response the nation agreed: "We will observe all that
Yahweh has decreed; we will obey" (Ex 24:7).

Peter's addressees are even more privileged. Nothing
less than the blood of Jesus Christ has sprinkled them.
How much more are they obligated to a life of obedience. Here is the dramatic grammar of the New Age:
the indicative statement of God's mercy linked with the
imperative of obedient commitment.

1 Peter 1:3–12
ABLE TO TAKE THE HEAT

3   Blessed be God the Father of our Lord Jesus
Christ, who in his great mercy has given us a new
birth as his sons, by raising Jesus Christ from the
4   dead, so that we have a sure hope ·and the promise of an inheritance that can never be spoiled or
soiled and never fade away, because it is being
5   kept for you in the heavens. ·Through your faith,
God's power will guard you until the salvation
which has been prepared is revealed at the end of
6   time. ·This is a cause of great joy for you, even
though you may for a short time have to bear
7   being plagued by all sorts of trials; ·so that, when
Jesus Christ is revealed, your faith will have been
tested and proved like gold—only it is more precious than gold, which is corruptible even though
it bears testing by fire—and then you will have
8   praise and glory and honor. ·You did not see him,
yet you love him; and still without seeing him, you
are already filled with a joy so glorious that it
9   cannot be described, because you believe; ·and
you are sure of the end to which your faith looks
forward, that is, the salvation of your souls.
10   It was this salvation that the prophets were
looking and searching so hard for; their prophecies were about the grace which was to come to
11   you. ·The Spirit of Christ which was in them foretold the sufferings of Christ and the glories that
would come after them, and they tried to find out
at what time and in what circumstances all this
12   was to be expected. ·It was revealed to them that
the news they brought of all the things which

have now been announced to you, by those who
preached to you the Good News through the Holy
Spirit sent from heaven, was for you and not
for themselves. Even the angels long to catch a
glimpse of these things.

✠

Again Peter records a majestic sentence (1:3–5) in
which he dramatically contrasts Christian anticipation
with the hopelessness and despair that are written on
numerous gravestones of secular antiquity.

The difference is due to the Christian understanding
of God, who has identity as "the Father of our Lord
Jesus Christ" (1:3). This is not sterile creedal statement. God's involvement in the life-and-death experience of Jesus is in fact the model for the understanding
of our own destiny.

Despite the fact that Jesus Christ is the Son of God
he underwent the degradation of a slave's death in our
behalf. But God raised him from the dead to be our
Lord and Master. God did not undergo all this anguish
merely to lighten the load of our lives until we die. On
the contrary, God raised up Jesus in order to offer us a
continuing prospect of life under Christ's Lordship beyond the darkness of the grave.

Peter's "hope" (1:3) is not a possibility on which
one accepts odds, but certainty about something in the
offing, guaranteed by God's own character and reputation. It's just a matter of time (1:5).

Under such circumstances—having such a marvel-
ously concerned God—we can shout for joy even in the
midst of reverses that challenge our confidence in
God's reliability (1:6).

One might think it would be sheer stupidity to risk
gold in fire. Yet it is done in the refining process, pre-

cisely in order to make the ore more valuable. Commitment to God is far more important than gold. When the unveiling of Jesus Christ takes place God wants to be even more proud of the believers than an artisan who looks with glee at the gold he has refined (1:7). In the meantime Jesus is not seen. Yet he is loved (1:8).

The phrase "salvation of your souls" (1:9) is to be understood in contrast to the hazards undergone by Christians as they live out their faith in a largely hostile world. Ultimately they will be released from it all. As often in the Bible, the word "soul" does not refer to something immortal but to the fundamental essence of a person—the real self or person.

Since the author writes quite probably near the end of the first century, he emphasizes the special privileges his recipients enjoy. The end of all things, and therefore the unveiling of Jesus Christ, are naturally closer to the present generation than to the earlier believers.

At various times prophetic voices spoke of an extraordinarily calamitous period of persecution that would usher in the termination of history (see Dn 12:1; Mk 13:8; and 4 Ezra 13:16–19, printed in some editions of the New English Bible). The technical term for this outpouring of misery is "the messianic woes." The phrase "the sufferings of Christ" (1:11) might therefore well be rendered: "the sufferings undergone for Christ."

One thing is certain, says Peter: They wrote for your benefit, not theirs (1:12)—that is, since you are in on the suffering, you will shortly be in on the glory (1:11).

STUDY QUESTION: In what ways does Peter show that Christians share in Israel's experiences?

1 Peter 1:13–21
MAKING WAVES WITH GOD

13   Free your minds, then, of encumbrances; control them, and put your trust in nothing but the grace that will be given you when Jesus Christ is
14 revealed. ·Do not behave in the way that you liked to before you learned the truth; make a habit of
15 obedience: ·be holy in all you do, since it is the
16 Holy One who has called you, ·and scripture says: Be holy, for I am holy.
17   If you are acknowledging as your Father one who has no favorites and judges everyone according to what he has done, you must be scrupulously careful as long as you are living away from
18 your home. ·Remember, the ransom that was paid to free you from the useless way of life your ancestors handed down was not paid in anything
19 corruptible, neither in silver nor gold, ·but in the precious blood of a lamb without spot or stain,
20 namely Christ; ·who, though known since before the world was made, has been revealed only in our
21 time, the end of the ages, for your sake. ·Through him you now have faith in God, who raised him from the dead and gave him glory for that very reason—so that you would have faith and hope in God.

✠

If Christianity has at times developed a reputation for ponderously slow movement in history, the fault is

not Peter's. People in his time hitched up their loosely
flowing robes so as to give their legs freedom of movement on the road. Similarly, when the Israelites left
Egypt, they adjusted their clothes for fast traveling (Ex
12:11). Peter evidently means: The worst posture for
the Church is to sit on its toga (1:13).

Like Israel at Sinai, Christians are committed to
obedience. This is far different from the way we were
programmed before our conversion. Ignorant of real
life with our Parent, we were once locked into the limited possibilities of various dominating desires, such as
impulse satisfactions and approval of the peer group at
all costs (1:14).

The opposite of impulsive conformity is "holy" living. Unfortunately this stained-glass term suggests
sanctimoniousness and even unworldliness, a performance level that has little to do with the realities of everyday experience. Nothing could be farther from
Peter's mind. Holiness is the cultivation through spirit,
mind, and action of the best possibilities for human
relationships. And God is the model for such approach
to life (1:15–16).

In his greeting Peter wrote about obedience. He has
just reaffirmed the identity of the new Exodus community as "obedient children." Now in 1:17–21 he proceeds to sharpen what it means to be a child in relation
to a Parent of such prestige as the Creator of the Universe and the Sponsor of the greatest act of deliverance
the world ever experienced before Jesus Christ. Just
because you can call God your Parent doesn't mean
you can pull strings. God refuses to be patronized.
Going on an exodus is serious business (1:17). Liberation is an invitation to challenging enterprises.

Centuries earlier Israel went out of Egypt carrying
jewelry of silver and gold they had requested from their
Egyptian neighbors (Ex 12:35). The climactic Exodus

at Calvary was far more costly to one of the participants. In the Sinai desert Israel was sprinkled with the blood of bulls. At Calvary the blood of the best that ever was, streamed down in behalf of all humanity (1:18–19).

By raising Jesus from the dead, God not only ratified his Son's credentials but also published the fact and invited the world back into the family. Christian faith is the response to God's well-planned interest in humanity's welfare. The Exodus was a great experience for Israel, but entry as a liberated people into the promised land of Canaan was the climax of their expectation. The latter-day Israel is guaranteed far more after its sojourn in the world (1:20–21).

Stripped of some of the sanctimonious unction his diction has experienced in translation, Peter's message is an invitation to uncommon performance. Like it or not, Exodus language is revolutionary terminology. To Pharaoh Moses was an arrogant activist, who was threatening the stable economic, political, religious, and social structures that had made Egypt an enviable power for more than a thousand years. And Peter's reminder to his own generation of Christians that they were rescued from traditional (ancestral) lifestyles is nothing less than a strong encouragement to make appropriate waves with God (1:18).

STUDY QUESTIONS: How does the main point made in 1:1–2 come out in 1:13–21? The commentary offers a definition of "holiness," but you, or each one in the group, might write out one of your own. What are some of the traditional lifestyles from which *you* have been rescued?

22 You have been obedient to the truth and purified your souls until you can love like brothers, in
sincerity; let your love for each other be real and
23 from the heart—·your new birth was not from any
mortal seed but from the everlasting word of the
24 living and eternal God. ·All flesh is grass and its
glory like the wild flower's. The grass withers, the
25 flower falls, ·but the word of the Lord remains for
ever. What is this word? It is the Good News that
has been brought to you.

1 Be sure, then, you are never spiteful, or de-
2 ceitful, or hypocritical, or envious and critical
of each other. ·You are newborn, and, like babies,
you should be hungry for nothing but milk—the
spiritual honesty which will help you to grow up
3 to salvation—·now that you have tasted the goodness of the Lord.

4 He is the living stone, rejected by men but
chosen by God and precious to him; set your-
5 selves close to him ·so that you too, the holy
priesthood that offers the spiritual sacrifices which
Jesus Christ has made acceptable to God, may be
6 living stones making a spiritual house. ·As scripture says: See how I lay in Zion a precious corner-
stone that I have chosen and the man who rests
7 his trust on it will not be disappointed. ·That
means that for you who are believers, it is precious; but for unbelievers, the stone rejected by
8 the builders has proved to be the keystone, ·a
stone to stumble over, a rock to bring men down.

They stumble over it because they do not believe
in the word; it was the fate in store for them.
9   But you are a chosen race, a royal priesthood,
a consecrated nation, a people set apart to sing the
praises of God who called you out of the darkness
10   into his wonderful light. ·Once you were not a
people at all and now you are the People of God;
once you were outside the mercy and now you
have been given mercy.

✝

Peter's approach to the future is no pizza-in-the-sky
or pot-for-the-masses theology. The whole idea of
God's redemptive activity is to liberate us from the oppressive games people play. Holiness is dedication to
openness in human relations, where YES means YES
and NO means NO, without patronizing maneuvering
for personal advantage. To love one another fervently
means to give up exploitative techniques (1:22).

The inheritance mentioned in 1:4 can never be
"spoiled," because we can call God our PARENT
(1:17), who has generated us anew through the Christian message (1:23). We are therefore committed to
obey our Parent, not the voices behind the traditional
patterns cited in 1:18. They have no future, says the
passage quoted in 1:24–25 from Isaiah 40:6–7. Para-
phrased, these words mean: Humanity left to its own
resources terminates in disaster. One's future is assured
only in connection with the Lord's Word.

With a slight alteration of his original text Peter focuses on Jesus Christ as the foundation figure in the
Christian fellowship (1:24–25). We grasp more clearly
now why Peter began this portion of his letter with a
warning against feigned relationships. God is our Parent, who now re-creates a new household, with Jesus

Christ as the center. Jealousy, exploitation, manipulation, and clever maneuvering for advantage do not
lead to enjoyable family life, and Peter reminds his
people that they are to have no part in these (2:1).
This reminder is not moralistic. On the contrary,
believers are growing up in the experience of salvation.
The glory after this present life will be in continuity
with present performance but at a much higher level of
expertise. To know Jesus Christ is to taste the future
and what it brings (2:2–3).

Family relationships suggest the picture of a house.
Therefore Peter proceeds to interpret his Exodus
model in terms of Israel's cult experience. God's house
would naturally be understood as a temple, but the
term is also applied to Israel, as in the phrase "house
of Israel." Therefore Peter describes his addressees as
stones who are becoming part of a structure that is
continually going up.

Since structure and function flow together in his metaphor, the living stones are all members of the Christian family. As priests and priestesses they are engaged
in offering themselves up as sacrifices. God accepts
these because of Jesus Christ, who holds the family together by virtue of his appointment as the linking stone
(2:4–5). The text says nothing about eligibility for the
later canonical office of the priesthood, which requires
specific gifts and expertise that are not possessed by
every Christian.

Written after the destruction of Jerusalem, our author's message would be especially consoling. In the
absence of the Second Temple, which was in ruins at
his time, many Jews who had acknowledged Jesus as
the Messiah would find in his words a way to continuity with their past. For Gentile converts the fresh
theology, supported by prophetic testimony (see Is

28:16), would open up immediate and unimpeded access to Israel's spiritual treasures (1 P 2:6).

At the same time the writer must account for the failure of the majority of Jews to realize their own expectations. After all, they were the Exodus people! What hope then is there for come-lately Gentiles? Peter answers: Those who rejected Jesus as the Messiah were disobedient. But the question of God's involvement cannot be ignored, therefore he adds: for which they were destined (2:7–8). Peter writes from a Jewish perspective. Nothing happens without God's involvement, who shows a hand even in disasters. That is very consoling, for what God permits God can also undo. The Gentiles should therefore profit from Israel's experience and offer an obedient response to God's call.

The identity of Israel is theirs. All the descriptive terms in 2:9 are drawn from Exodus 19:6 and 23:22. As selectees for new identity they are not to bask in their VIP status. Instead they are to proclaim God's marvelous character and wonderfully generous action in behalf of humanity and especially of those within the Christian family. Once it was said of Israel that they were changed from No-People to People-of-God (Ho 1:9). The same can be said of the Gentiles: Once-without-Mercy, Now-Recipients-of-Mercy (2:9–10).

STUDY QUESTIONS: What does it mean to "grow up in the experience of salvation"? In what ways are *all* Christians priests and priestesses?

1 Peter 2:11 – 3:12
JUST PASSING THROUGH

11 I urge you, my dear people, while you are visitors and pilgrims to keep yourselves free from the
12 selfish passions that attack the soul. ·Always behave honorably among pagans so that they can see your good works for themselves and, when the day of reckoning comes, give thanks to God for the things which now make them denounce you as criminals.

13 For the sake of the Lord, accept the authority of every social institution: the emperor, as the
14 supreme authority, ·and the governors as commissioned by him to punish criminals and praise good
15 citizenship. ·God wants you to be good citizens, so as to silence what fools are saying in their ig-
16 norance. ·You are slaves of no one except God, so behave like free men, and never use your freedom
17 as an excuse for wickedness. ·Have respect for everyone and love for our community; fear God and honor the emperor.

18 Slaves must be respectful and obedient to their masters, not only when they are kind and gentle
19 but also when they are unfair. ·You see, there is some merit in putting up with the pains of un-earned punishment if it is done for the sake of
20 God ·but there is nothing meritorious in taking a beating patiently if you have done something wrong to deserve it. The merit, in the sight of God, is in bearing it patiently when you are punished after doing your duty.

21 This, in fact, is what you were called to do, because Christ suffered for you and left an example
22 for you to follow the way he took. ·He had not

done anything wrong, and there had been no per-
²³ jury in his mouth. ·He was insulted and did not
retaliate with insults; when he was tortured he
made no threats but he put his trust in the right-
²⁴ eous judge. ·He was bearing our faults in his own
body on the cross, so that we might die to our
faults and live for holiness; through his wounds
²⁵ you have been healed. ·You had gone astray like
sheep but now you have come back to the shepherd and guardian of your souls.

¹ 3 In the same way, wives should be obedient to
their husbands. Then, if there are some husbands who have not yet obeyed the word, they
may find themselves won over, without a word
² spoken, by the way their wives behave, ·when
they see how faithful and conscientious they are.
³ Do not dress up for show: doing up your hair,
⁴ wearing gold bracelets and fine clothes; ·all this
should be inside, in a person's heart, imperishable:
the ornament of a sweet and gentle disposition—
⁵ this is what is precious in the sight of God. ·That
was how the holy women of the past dressed
themselves attractively—they hoped in God and
⁶ were tender and obedient to their husbands; ·like
Sarah, who was obedient to Abraham, and called
him her lord. You are now her children, as long
as you live good lives and do not give way to fear
or worry.

⁷   In the same way, husbands must always treat
their wives with consideration in their life together, respecting a woman as one who, though
she may be the weaker partner, is equally an heir
to the life of grace. This will stop anything from
coming in the way of your prayers.

⁸   Finally: you should all agree among yourselves and be sympathetic; love the brothers, have
⁹ compassion and be self-effacing. ·Never pay back
one wrong with another, or an angry word with
another one; instead, pay back with a blessing.
That is what you are called to do, so that you
¹⁰ inherit a blessing yourself. ·Remember: Anyone
who wants to have a happy life and to enjoy
prosperity must banish malice from his tongue,

11 deceitful conversation from his lips; ·he must
   never yield to evil but must practice good; he must
12 seek peace and pursue it. ·Because the face of the
   Lord frowns on evil men, but the eyes of the Lord
   are turned toward the virtuous, his ears to their
   cry.

✠

After his telling use of the Exodus model, Peter
turns to the Exile as paradigm for expansion of his
theme of obedience.

Like their ancestor Abraham, Israelites found themselves in a strange land after the fall of Jerusalem in
587 B.C. Christians, invited as they are to uncommon
performance levels, would necessarily feel like visitors
to a foreign country. Their endeavors to maintain the
highest standards of ethics might well expose them to
charges of threatening the stability of social, economic,
political, and religious structures. But one day God will
hold court, and the truth will out. Yet some of their enemies will have second thoughts and be converted
when they continue to see the remarkable integrity of
Christians whom they once vilified. On the Day of
Judgment they will confess that they saw God's character unfold before them in the words and deeds of those
whom they accused (2:11–12).

Obedience is his theme, and Peter begins with the
toughest problem of all. How does one who aims to be
obedient to God relate to the real world with its many
authoritative structures? Here theology hits the street.

To understand his line of argument it is necessary to
note that the problem, as Peter sees it, is not about the
validity of structures and institutions as such—slavery,
for example—but what one does when a structure demands decisions that are incompatible with one's pro-

fession of Christianity. Answer: Do your duty, but
when there is conflict of interest, opt for God.

Peter begins with the political structures, and his description is far removed from some of the quietistic in-
terpretations given to his words. First of all, the highest
authorities and their representatives owe their office to
God and are accountable to God. It is their responsibility to move against those who exploit others, and
to encourage those who promote society's best interests
(2:13–14). By obeying God, the highest constituted
authority, Christians cannot fail to meet their obligations to the State. Such perspective validates resort to
civil disobedience, but the counsel is not to be used as
a cover for personal agendas that jeopardize the interests of society. As a community in the Exodus tradition, Christians are under orders from the Very Highest
Authority (2:15–17).

In 2:18–25 Peter tackles the touchy problem of
slavery. Aristotle defined a slave as a "tool," a thing to
be used at the will of the owner. Roman law offered
some amelioration of a slave's lot. Not a few of them
managed to secure their freedom, and in some instances even rose to high positions in the political and
economic structures. But the general picture, as for-
merly in the United States, was one of dismal and de-
moralizing circumstances for slave, master, and mis-
tress. Looking in from the outside it is almost
impossible to imagine the moral dilemmas posed by
non-Christian households where demands made on
Christian female slaves might at times run counter to
their moral standards. To such people, caught in a real
world not of their making, Peter offered an attractive
route to personal identity.

To know that one is first of all the slave of God introduces a strong measure of challenge in the face of
demands that run counter to one's primary allegiance.

Obviously, says Peter, you will have to suffer the consequences of affirming your identity in the face of stupid or malicious masters. Civil disobedience carries a price. But that is their problem, not yours (2:18–19).

It is difficult for Westerners, long accustomed to artistic and liturgical reproduction of the cross, to appreciate the effect that Peter's reference to the suffering of Jesus Christ would have on slaves of the first century. Ordinarily suffering and death were the lots of slaves who were engaged in subversive activity against the system. Spartacus led a slave revolt, and the countryside was silhouetted with bodies on crosses, grim reminders that such tactics did not pay.

The proclamation of a crucified Savior was in effect the constant waving of a red flag under the nose of Roman imperial society. It was also a constant reminder to Rome that its vaunted sense of justice had gone astray in the case of Jesus, who was declared innocent by the Emperor's own prefect, Pontius Pilate. In brief, the mode of Jesus' death was a powerful symbol of moral remonstrance against *all* that is dehumanizing in history. In the face of injustice it is still possible to affirm justice—sometimes at a high price, as Dr. Martin Luther King and others have discovered (2:20–25).

Atlanta Braves' catcher Bruce Benedict was dejected when his pitcher, Phil Niekro, made a record four wild pitches in one inning. Niekro's knuckleball was simply too much for Benedict that day. "I'm pretty down right now," Benedict said after the game, "but nobody will feel sorry for you in this league. You are paid to catch knuckleballs." Translated into 1 Peter language one can hear the text saying: "God made no promise to keep you out of danger when you were called to share the family circle."

Peter's close association of the problems of women

with those of slaves is indicative of his perceptive empathy. Unlike their Roman peers, who enjoyed considerable freedom after their prepuberty confinement, women in the provinces of Asia Minor would feel the tighter strictures imposed by Middle Eastern traditions. It was expected that a woman's will would generally coincide with that of her husband. This meant that if a wife became a Christian while married to a non-Christian, she could expect conflict, especially in religious obligations.

Peter strikes a blow for her liberation by emphasizing that she should not be intimidated when her prior allegiance to God exposes her to such conflict. At the same time, if her husband has any brains at all he will recognize the value of a woman who puts a warm and faithful personality ahead of material interests (3:3–4). Quite evidently Peter's language does not support the caricature of "the total woman," nor is the text to be used as ammunition against the Avon Ladies. The reference to Sarah (3:6), Abraham's wife, is in keeping with the theme of believers as constituting the end-time Israel.

Since men generally controlled the power structures, Peter reserved them for final mention. Christian males would need to exercise unusual prudence and responsibility in dealing with the female slaves under their care. The translators infer the word "wives" (3:7) from the address at 3:1, but Peter does not narrowly specify, and his delicate phrasing suggests that females in general are under discussion. Whether their female slaves were Christian or not, a Christian master is to recognize their relative defenselessness in the face of superior power that is also endowed by traditional sanction. That slaves should be considered worthy of "honor" (3:7)—they are included under the word "all" used at 2:17—was itself a revolutionary concept.

Christian husbands are to recognize that their social, political, and economic structures put wives at a disadvantage. Oppressive policies, our writer adds, can block one's prayers (3:7; see 3:12; Ps 34:16).

Peter could go on and examine all possible relationships in society. Instead he compresses all possibilities of human relations into one sentence (3:8–9) and underscores his appeal for open and caring relationships with a citation from Psalm 34:13–17. This passage concludes with a reinforcement of the importance of fairness or justice. God looks with favor on those who are fair to the powerless (3:10–11). Insensitivity toward the weak can keep one's petitions from getting through (see 3:7). However, the fair and just person (rendered "virtuous" by JB) will always find God ready to listen (3:12).

From this sequence of instructions it is apparent that affirmative answers to six questions will certify the superior quality of a relationship involving especially the sexual factor:

1. Is it marked by faithfulness and commitment?

2. Is it enriching of the participants?

3. Is it characterized by honesty and openness?

4. Is it socially responsible?

5. Is it joyous?

6. Is it liberating of the self and the other?

STUDY QUESTIONS: How are you as a church member today a threat to "social, economic, political, and religious structures"? What are the ways in which people today are turned into "things"?

1 Peter 3:13 – 4:6
TABLES WILL BE TURNED

¹³ No one can hurt you if you are determined to
¹⁴ do only what is right; ·if you do have to suffer for
being good, you will count it a blessing. There is
¹⁵ no need to be afraid or to worry about them. ·Simply reverence the Lord Christ in your hearts, and
always have your answer ready for people who
ask you the reason for the hope that you all have.
¹⁶ But give it with courtesy and respect and with a
clear conscience, so that those who slander you
when you are living a good life in Christ may be
proved wrong in the accusations that they bring.
¹⁷ And if it is the will of God that you should suffer,
it is better to suffer for doing right than for doing
wrong.
¹⁸ Why, Christ himself, innocent though he was,
had died once for sins, died for the guilty, to lead
us to God. In the body he was put to death, in the
¹⁹ spirit he was raised to life, ·and, in the spirit, he
²⁰ went to preach to the spirits in prison. ·Now it
was long ago, when Noah was still building that
ark which saved only a small group of eight people "by water," and when God was still waiting
patiently, that these spirits refused to believe.
²¹ That water is a type of the baptism which saves
you now, and which is not the washing off of
physical dirt but a pledge made to God from a
good conscience, through the resurrection of Jesus
²² Christ, ·who has entered heaven and is at God's
right hand, now that he has made the angels and
Dominations and Powers his subjects.

¹ **4** Think of what Christ suffered in this life, and
then arm yourselves with the same resolution
that he had: anyone who in this life has bodily suf-
² fering has broken with sin, ·because for the rest of
his life on earth he is not ruled by human passions
³ but only by the will of God. ·You spent quite long
enough in the past living the sort of life that pagans live, behaving indecently, giving way to your
passions, drinking all the time, having wild parties
and drunken orgies and degrading yourselves by
⁴ following false gods. ·So people cannot understand why you no longer hurry off with them to
join this flood which is rushing down to ruin, and
⁵ then they begin to spread libels about you. ·They
will have to answer for it in front of the judge
who is ready to judge the living and the dead.
⁶ And because he is their judge too, the dead had
to be told the Good News as well, so that though,
in their life on earth, they had been through the
judgment that comes to all humanity, they might
come to God's life in the spirit.

✠

1 Peter 3:13–17

Ordinarily goodness and fair dealing elicit favorable
response (3:13). But, acknowledges Peter, you may at
times have to suffer for your convictions (3:14). In
such cases don't lose your nerve! The bottom line of
obedience is loyalty to the One Lord and Master—
Christ. If anyone wonders why you are willing to take
such risks, tell the truth. But do it without arrogance
and unnecessary provocation (3:16). Just be sure you
don't blame God for homegrown suffering that has
nothing to do with Christian conviction (3:15–17).

1 Peter 3:18–4:6

With verse 18, Peter moves into theological waters
that have swamped many an interpreter. The difficulty
of 3:18–4:6 stems chiefly from the lack by today's
reader of the ready associations that made it perfectly
clear to the original recipients. But once the main
thread is spotted—assurance of victory over the scoffers
—the full pattern begins to emerge.

"Eat, drink, and be merry, for tomorrow we die!"
appears to be the slogan of the unconverted (4:3).
And they seem to be in the right, for Christians who
boast of a resurrected Leader die one after the other.
After their pains to maintain high moral standards,
they suffer social and economic reprisal in the bargain
during their brief lifetimes.

Being known as a follower of Jesus Christ in the first
century did in fact make one about as popular as a
shark off Daytona Beach at the height of the swimming
season in our time. Christianity put question marks
over much of society (4:3), and reprisals were as pre-
dictable as grasshoppers in a field of standing grain.
But the early Christians were not alone in this respect.
Also Jesus was innocent, yet the death he suffered appeared to cast him in the role of the most lawless in society. To highlight this contrast Peter draws on the
story of the Flood.

According to the noncanonical *Book of Enoch* (see
Jude 14), the population at the time of the Flood was
horribly immoral. They were the kind of people with
whom Jesus was classified when he went to the realm
of the dead (1 P 3:18–19). From a purely human perspective he was a criminal of the first order, and the
manner of his death appeared to confirm the verdict.
But God reversed appearances, and Jesus was given

life at a level different from the purely biological—the
level of the *spirit* (3:19). Under this twofold circumstance—on the one hand, of apparent defeat, and on
the other, of real victory over death—he served as
God's agent in making a royal proclamation
(3:18–19), which the translators render "preach." Far
from being the archcriminal he appeared to be at the
moment of his death, he is the One ratified by God as
the agent of salvation for all the world.

The story of the Flood offers Peter further opportunity to console the Christian communities. Like Noah's
relatives, who were outnumbered by scoffing unbelievers, Christians are a tiny minority in a world ripe
for judgment.

Eight people made it through the Flood. Ironically,
the very instrument of destruction for the majority of
humanity became the means of rescue for a tiny minority (3:20). Likewise the water of baptism saves Christians. In a sense it constitutes death of all that once
seemed to spell life. At the same time it marks rebirth
into the New Age. At baptism we pledge ourselves to
serve God faithfully, and the resurrected Lord provides
the support system for the keeping of that pledge. After
having suffered to the uttermost he became second in
command. Now all conceivable power structures, including those to which Christians are subject (2:13,
18; 3:1) are subject to his review and control. Therefore Christians need not hesitate to affirm authority
structures within the limits of their allegiance to Jesus
Christ. But when power demands more than it has a
right to ask, Christians may suffer for their refusal to
grant Caesar what belongs only to God (3:21–22).

In 1 Peter 4:1–6 the author carries out the theme of
apparent defeat followed by victory. Skillfully he high-
lights his line of thought through a series of moral in-
dictments that suggest the popular epitaph noted

earlier: EAT, DRINK, AND BE MERRY, FOR
TOMORROW WE DIE! That is the taunting advice of
unbelievers. Despite all your talk about a new life, you
Christians still help fill the cemeteries!

In response Peter says that those who scoff at the
Christians' refusal to identify with the unbelievers' last-
fling philosophy are in fact mortgaging themselves to
the mortician. They are pouring out their own *flood*
(4:4) of iniquity, and like the Great Flood it will
drown *them*. You who are identified with Jesus Christ
are really alive. They may look at the corpses among
you and say, "See, they died, too." But just as Jesus
was made alive in respect to his spirit, so the departed
in the community now live on a transcendent level
whose perspective is known in depth only by God. For
this reason the Gospel was proclaimed to those Christians who have been buried (4:6).

STUDY QUESTIONS: Some commentators conclude that
3:18 – 4:6 teaches "universalism,"
and that Jesus proclaimed the Gospel to the Flood victims. What do
you think about this? What are the
reasons for your conclusions?

1 Peter 4:7–19
THE END IS NEAR

7 Everything will soon come to an end, so, to
8 pray better, keep a calm and sober mind. ·Above
all, never let your love for each other grow in-
9 sincere, since love covers over many a sin. ·Wel-
come each other into your houses without grum-
10 bling. ·Each one of you has received a special
grace, so, like good stewards responsible for all
these different graces of God, put yourselves at
11 the service of others. ·If you are a speaker, speak
in words which seem to come from God; if you
are a helper, help as though every action was
done at God's orders; so that in everything God
may receive the glory, through Jesus Christ, since
to him alone belong all glory and power for ever
and ever. Amen.

12 My dear people, you must not think it unac-
countable that you should be tested by fire. There
is nothing extraordinary in what has happened to
13 you. ·If you can have some share in the sufferings
of Christ, be glad, because you will enjoy a much
14 greater gladness when his glory is revealed. ·It is
a blessing for you when they insult you for bearing the name of Christ, because it means that you
have the Spirit of glory, the Spirit of God resting
15 on you. ·None of you should ever deserve to suffer for being a murderer, a thief, a criminal or
16 an informer; ·but if anyone of you should suffer
for being a Christian, then he is not to be ashamed
of it; he should thank God that he has been called
17 one. ·The time has come for the judgment to begin at the household of God; and if what we know

now is only the beginning, what will it be when it comes down to those who refuse to believe God's
18 Good News? ·If it is hard for a good man to be saved, what will happen to the wicked and to
19 sinners? ·So even those whom God allows to suffer must trust themselves to the constancy of the creator and go on doing good.

✠

1 Peter 4:7–11

Sincerity is the pervading theme of 4:7–11. In contrast to the self-indulgent and irresponsible lifestyle described in 4:3, Christians are to keep cool heads and pray for fidelity to God's expectations. At first sight it might be thought that love is a cover-up operation. But the Semitic understanding is that love acts in such a way that a cover-up becomes unnecessary. Love is openness to the other (4:7–8).

Being in the minority, Christians needed a reliable support system. The hospitality here described is not the cherry-and-olives, now-it's-our-turn syndrome, but reception of the needy, the lonely, and the oppressed—and without the grudging attitude that ordinarily accompanies advertisement of such need. Endowments of personality, economic advantage, and talent are to be used not for self-indulgence and exploitation of others but to magnify God's reputation (4:9–11).

1 Peter 4:12–19

Peter's words offer no endorsement of a theology that interprets Christianity as a trip to worldly success. On the contrary, Christians who put into question some of the performance patterns of the systems and struc-

tures that surround them will be quite certain to invite
hostility, and not seldom from within their own ranks.
But the encounter serves as a refining process in which
the genuine article is separated from the chaff (4:17).
That in itself is a consolation. If judgment begins with
the family of believers, God will surely mean business
throughout the universe. It may appear that the wicked
have the last laugh. Yet they will be the first to weep
(4:18). And Christians can submit their case to God
even in the face of disaster. "Trust me," says the Creator (4:19).

STUDY QUESTION: From your own experience, in what
                ways have you seen judgment be-
                ginning at God's own "household"?

1 Peter 5:1–14
COLLEGIALITY IN THE FAITH

¹ Now I have something to tell your elders: I am an elder myself, and a witness to the sufferings of Christ, and with you I have a share in ² the glory that is to be revealed. ·Be the shepherds of the flock of God that is entrusted to you: watch over it, not simply as a duty but gladly, because God wants it; not for sordid money, but because ³ you are eager to do it. ·Never be a dictator over any group that is put in your charge, but be an ex⁴ ample that the whole flock can follow. ·When the chief shepherd appears, you will be given the crown of unfading glory.

⁵ To the rest of you I say: do what the elders tell you, and all wrap yourselves in humility to be servants of each other, because God refuses the ⁶ proud and will always favor the humble. ·Bow down, then, before the power of God now, and ⁷ he will raise you up on the appointed day; ·unload all your worries on to him, since he is looking ⁸ after you. ·Be calm but vigilant, because your enemy the devil is prowling around like a roaring ⁹ lion, looking for someone to eat. ·Stand up to him, strong in faith and in the knowledge that your brothers all over the world are suffering the ¹⁰ same things. ·You will have to suffer only for a little while: the God of all grace who called you to eternal glory in Christ will see that all is well again: he will confirm, strengthen and support ¹¹ you. ·His power lasts for ever and ever. Amen.
¹² I write these few words to you through Silvanus, who is a brother I know I can trust, to en-

courage you never to let go this true grace of
God to which I bear witness.
13   Your sister in Babylon, who is with you among
the chosen, sends you greetings; so does my son,
Mark.
14   Greet one another with a kiss of love.
Peace to you all who are in Christ.

✠

1 Peter 5:1–5

In view of the perils facing Christian pockets of resistance to evil, Christians require pastoral leadership
of high quality. Collegiality in suffering is a prime re-
quirement, undergirded by genuine interest in people as
opposed to pursuit of private advantage. Bishops and
pastors do not own the flock. It belongs to God. Far
from viewing their offices as media for clout, they are
to be models of humility. The honors and prestige that
the world offers will fade with time. In an echo of 1:4,
Peter says that the Chief Shepherd—Jesus Christ—will
award the unfading wreath of glory (5:1–5).

1 Peter 5:6–11

Through the practice of everyday humility Christians
are to become experts in it so that they may be able to
bear up under the mighty hand of God (5:5–7). This
means that God will ultimately win the battles for
them. At the same time we are not to underestimate the
opposition. Mistake it not, there is a demonic dimension to the hostility experienced by Christ's followers.
"The devil" does not hesitate to exploit possibilities for
oppression in social systems and power structures.
Never mind; "stand up to him" and be counted (5:8).

It is very easy to fall into the trap of thinking that others are exempt from the consequences of confessing Christ. Peter therefore borrows a standard theme of consolation used in antiquity: You are not being picked on, and your problem is not unusual (5:9). Besides, it's only temporary. And God, who permits it, will see you through it (5:9–11).

1 Peter 5:12–14

The name Silas suggests some point of mediation between the Apostle Peter and the addressees of this Epistle. The astounding truth is that a state of affairs that at first glance seems to suggest a misplaced faith and confidence in God is in reality the *true* grace. TO BE CONFRONTED WITH DISASTER IS EVIDENCE OF DIVINE FAVOR (5:12). Nor are the addressees alone. Their associates in "Babylon" greet them. With this metaphorical place name the author brings the Israel-Exile theme full circle. "Sister-in-Babylon" is a compressed term for Israel-in-Exile, temporarily away from the promised land (5:13). Love and peace are the twin notes of hope. They compose the song for the New Age (5:14).

STUDY QUESTIONS: What are the best antidotes against anticlericalism? How would you define the "demonic" for a person on the street? Do you think it is possible in today's world to affirm the reality of the "devil"? What are your reasons for your last two answers?

2 Peter
The Second Letter of Peter

INTRODUCTION

God's image as a philanthropist is seldom projected in Christian conversation. The Epistle of Second Peter is unique in its manner of expressing this aspect of God's personality.

Because of the Apostle Peter's prestige, a number of writings were associated with his name. Like 1 Peter, the second that bears his name originated very late in the first century.

Because of its polemical tone, and partly because of a general failure on the part of commentators to recognize the literary ingenuity of the writer, 2 Peter has not received the attention it deserves. I hope this commentary will offer some remedy.

From at least two points of view 2 Peter is worthy of special response: (1) It demonstrates how Christians can identify at the highest levels of a humanistic outlook, without diminution of their claim to larger perspectives. (2) It encourages Christians to combine end-of-the-world thinking with in-depth involvement in responsible decision-making.

I invite you to participate in the study of this remarkable document.

2 Peter 1:1–2
IMPERIAL AUTHORITY

¹ **1** From Simeon Peter, servant and apostle of
Jesus Christ; to all who treasure the same faith
as ourselves, given through the righteousness of
² our God and Savior Jesus Christ. ·May you have
more and more grace and peace as you come to
know our Lord more and more.

✠

Our writer's self-identification as a slave (JB "servant") and apostle draws attention to the imperial
prestige of Jesus Christ (1:1). Since the addressees belong to a generation of Christians for whom the apostolic period is but a memory, the writer assures them
that they share a privilege of faith-commitment on the
same terms as the first-generation Christians.

2 Peter 1:3–11
PHILANTHROPISTS OF THE NEW AGE

³ By his divine power, he has given us all the things that we need for life and for true devotion, bringing us to know God himself, who has called ⁴ us by his own glory and goodness. ·In making these gifts, he has given us the guarantee of something very great and wonderful to come: through them you will be able to share the divine nature and to escape corruption in a world that is sunk ⁵ in vice. ·But to attain this, you will have to do your utmost yourselves, adding goodness to the faith that you have, understanding to your good-⁶ ness, ·self-control to your understanding, patience to your self-control, true devotion to your pa-⁷ tience, ·kindness toward your fellow men to your ⁸ devotion, and, to this kindness, love. ·If you have a generous supply of these, they will not leave you ineffectual or unproductive: they will bring you to a real knowledge of our Lord Jesus Christ. ⁹ But without them a man is blind or else short-sighted; he has forgotten how his past sins were ¹⁰ washed away. ·Brothers, you have been called and chosen: work all the harder to justify it. If you do all these things there is no danger that you ¹¹ will ever fall away. ·In this way you will be granted admittance into the eternal kingdom of our Lord and Savior Jesus Christ.

✠

Up and down the Mediterranean world, Christians could see huge slabs of rock on which were inscribed laudatory dedications and decrees in honor of public benefactors. One of these reads:

> Whereas Theocles . . . of Meliboea has proved himself a perfect gentleman . . . and has rendered exceptional service to our citizens . . . be it resolved that Theocles be declared our public friend and representative; that he be granted exemption from whatever imposts our city has authority to exact and be free to come and go both in war and in peace, without formality of treaty; that he enjoy the privilege of a front seat at the Games; and that he be officially recognized with the rest of our city's representatives.

The two parts—preamble and resolution—are standard in thousands of similar decrees.

In his brilliant adaptation of the Greco-Roman-benefactor theme, Peter first of all delivers a preamble in praise of the princely generosity of God and Jesus Christ (1:3–4). Eastern potentates were highly praised when they delivered on their promises. God is even more reliable and enables us to share in the divine nature: performance of the highest order. Far from being a hindrance to real living, God's deliverance from a style of life that can spell only destruction is God's supreme gift.

Verses 5–11 correspond to the grateful response that popular assemblies would make to philanthropists. Quite adroitly Peter turns the recipients of divine benefactions into benefactors. The word rendered "goodness" (1:5) was the customary term applied to public-spirited citizens who displayed the highest standards of excellence in discharge of civic responsibility and in personal rectitude. Whereas the laudatory inscriptions were erected in honor of a relatively few citizens in proportion to the general populace,

Peter expects every Christian to qualify for such a citation from God.

Climaxing the components of distinguished service are the terms "true devotion," "kindness," and "love" (1:6–7). The first of these expresses the vertical dimension of one's relation to God. The other two define the horizontal dimension of relationships with fellow human beings. One could well say of persons who claimed to be Christians but lacked these characteristics, that they did not put a very high value on the divine philanthropy of forgiveness (1:8–9).

Peter's verdict was calculated to make an impression in a world that took a dim view of short memories about beneficence (verse 9). On the other hand, those who perform in a public-spirited fashion will be escorted as VIP's into the Great King's very presence.

STUDY QUESTION: Use whatever reference work you have at hand and locate a definition of "humanism." In what way does 2 Peter dispel the notion that Christianity is not concerned about human interests and ideals?

2 Peter 1:12–21
EYEWITNESSES OF JESUS' MAJESTY

¹² That is why I am continually recalling the same truths to you, even though you already ¹³ know them and firmly hold them. ·I am sure it is my duty, as long as I am in this tent, to keep stir- ¹⁴ ring you up with reminders, ·since I know the time for taking off this tent is coming soon, as our ¹⁵ Lord Jesus Christ foretold to me. ·And I shall take great care that after my own departure you will still have a means to recall these things to memory.

¹⁶ It was not any cleverly invented myths that we were repeating when we brought you the knowl- edge of the power and the coming of our Lord Jesus Christ; we had seen his majesty for our- ¹⁷ selves. ·He was honored and glorified by God the Father, when the Sublime Glory itself spoke to him and said, "This is my Son, the Beloved; he ¹⁸ enjoys my favor." ·We heard this ourselves, spoken from heaven, when we were with him on the holy mountain.

¹⁹ So we have confirmation of what was said in prophecies; and you will be right to depend on prophecy and take it as a lamp for lighting a way through the dark until the dawn comes and the ²⁰ morning star rises in your minds. ·At the same time, we must be most careful to remember that the interpretation of scriptural prophecy is never ²¹ a matter for the individual. ·Why? Because no prophecy ever came from man's initiative. When men spoke for God it was the Holy Spirit that moved them.

✠

In support of the grandiloquent diction he has just used concerning Jesus Christ, the writer takes his readers back into history and makes them participants with Peter, James, and John, who once viewed the transfiguration of Jesus (see Mk 9:2–9; Mt 17:1–8; Lk 9:28–36). On that occasion God dramatically affirmed the status of the Son (2 P 1:17).

The words recited on the mountain of transfiguration ratify the prophetic word (1:19) concerning the windup of history. Jesus' majesty as seen by the apostles was a preview of the majesty he will display on his return at the end of time. Moreover, the prophetic word is not the product of human creativity. Like the voice that spoke at the transfiguration, the prophetic word of Scripture is of divine origin. Prophets do not express their own ideas. They are the mouthpieces of the Holy Spirit. To interpret them correctly one must also have the Spirit.

With this ratification of the Sacred Scriptures, the author prepares his public for the indictment of false teachers who question traditional Christian teaching about the approaching end of all things.

STUDY QUESTION: How does 2 Peter help Christians protect themselves against perpetrating arbitrary interpretation of the Scriptures?

2 Peter 2
COUNTERREVOLUTIONARIES

¹ 2 As there were false prophets in the past history of our people, so you too will have your false teachers, who will insinuate their own disruptive views and disown the Master who purchased their freedom. They will destroy them-
² selves very quickly; ·but there will be many who copy their shameful behavior, and the Way of Truth will be brought into disrepute on their ac-
³ count. ·They will eagerly try to buy you for themselves with insidious speeches, but for them the Condemnation, pronounced so long ago, is at its work already, and Destruction is not asleep.
⁴ When angels sinned, God did not spare them: he sent them down to the underworld and consigned them to the dark underground caves to be
⁵ held there till the day of Judgment. ·Nor did he spare the world in ancient times: it was only Noah he saved, the preacher of righteousness, along with seven others, when he sent the Flood over a dis-
⁶ obedient world. ·The cities of Sodom and Gomorrah, these too he condemned and reduced to ashes; he destroyed them completely, as a warning to
⁷ anybody lacking reverence in the future; ·he rescued Lot, however, a holy man who had been sickened by the shameless way in which these vile
⁸ people behaved—·for that holy man, living among them, was outraged in his good soul by the crimes
⁹ that he saw and heard of every day. ·These are all examples of how the Lord can rescue the good from the ordeal, and hold the wicked for their
¹⁰ punishment until the day of Judgment, ·especially

those who are governed by their corrupt bodily
desires and have no respect for authority.

Such self-willed people with no reverence are
not afraid of offending against the glorious ones,
11 but the angels in their greater strength and power
make no complaint or accusation against them in
12 front of the Lord. ·All the same, these people who
only insult anything that they do not understand
are not reasoning beings, but simply animals born
to be caught and killed, and they will quite certainly destroy themselves by their own work of
13 destruction, ·and get their reward of evil for the
evil that they do. They are unsightly blots on your
society: men whose only object is dissipation all
day long, and they amuse themselves deceiving
you even when they are your guests at a meal;
14 with their eyes always looking for adultery, men
with an infinite capacity for sinning, they will se-
duce any soul which is at all unstable. Greed is
the one lesson their minds have learned. They are
15 under a curse. ·They have left the right path and
wandered off to follow the path of Balaam son of
Beor, who thought he could profit best by sinning,
16 until he was called to order for his faults. The
dumb donkey put a stop to that prophet's mad-
17 ness when it talked like a man. ·People like this
are dried-up rivers, fogs swirling in the wind, and
the dark underworld is the place reserved for
18 them. ·With their high-flown talk, which is all
hollow, they tempt back the ones who have only
just escaped from paganism, playing on their
19 bodily desires with debaucheries. ·They may
promise freedom but they themselves are slaves,
slaves to corruption; because if anyone lets himself be dominated by anything, then he is a slave
20 to it; ·and anyone who has escaped the pollution
of the world once by coming to know our Lord
and savior Jesus Christ, and who then allows himself to be entangled by it a second time and mas-
tered, will end up in a worse state than he began
21 in. ·It would even have been better for him never
to have learned the way of holiness, than to know
it and afterward desert the holy rule that was en-
22 trusted to him. ·What he has done is exactly as the

> proverb rightly says: The dog goes back to his own
> vomit and: When the sow has been washed, it
> wallows in the mud.

✠

As does the writer of the Letter of Jude, our author
adopts the vigorous invective of diatribe, a popular
form of moralistic writing and streetpreaching in antiquity.

From our writer's perspective, people who challenge
apostolic teaching of the world's early termination are
imperiling a basic motivational force for Christian morality (2:1–2). To undergird his argument, the writer
introduces two sets of examples: (1) The rebel angels,
the people of Noah's time, and Noah and his family
(2:4–5); (2) the cities of the Plain and Lot (2:6–7).
Each of these sets consists of contrasting personalities,
one side bad and the other good. Each set also contrasts the fate of the participants. The rebel angels, the
world at the time of the Flood, and Sodom and Gomorrah experienced judgments that are previews of the
Last Day.

Those who willfully oppose God's purposes will one
day discover what Antonia Makarova learned to her
sorrow. Known as "Machine-gun Tanya," she killed
scores of prisoners as a political executioner. When she
was sentenced to death, an editor commented: "She
thought she could walk away from her past."

Good Noah and Lot typify God's rescue of the
believers from the perils of that day.

Details on most of our writer's cast of characters for
his second chapter are recorded in the commentary on
Jude. Here it is important to note that our writer corre-
lates the theme of the end of the world with Christian
moral responsibility.

Apparently the false teachers under discussion questioned the value of books that dealt with the theme of the end of the world. These books are classified as Apocalyptic, and one of them—the *Book of Enoch*—was cited by Jude. The *Book of Enoch* describes the fall of the rebel angels and events leading up to the end of the world. Our writer excoriates scoffers who dismiss the noncanonical apocalyptic tradition (2:10) but does not follow Jude in quoting directly from it. Our writer prefers to stress the more generally accepted prophetic Scriptural word (1:20–21) and the Lord's own directive as communicated by the apostles (3:2).

To illustrate the intimate connection between morality and expectation of an end-time judgment, the writer cites the story of Balaam, whose greed is typical of the materialism infecting the false teachers.

From the language used in 2:18–19, it also appears that the false teachers have misread and misapplied Paul's letters in which the apostle to the Gentiles had announced freedom from the Law of Moses (for example, see Ga 5:1). Our writer makes explicit reference to their distortion at 3:14–16.

STUDY QUESTIONS: At times Church leaders have used passages like 2 Peter to discourage introduction of fresh knowledge and theological viewpoint. What antidote does 2 Peter offer against such obscurantism? What *is* a false teacher in his book?

2 Peter 3
NEW CREATION

¹ 3 My friends, this is my second letter to you, and in both of them I have tried to awaken a true understanding in you by giving you a re- ² minder: ·recalling to you what was said in the past by the holy prophets and the commandments of the Lord and savior which you were given by the apostles.

³ We must be careful to remember that during the last days there are bound to be people who will be scornful, the kind who always please them- selves in what they do, and they will make fun of ⁴ the promise ·and ask, "Well, where is this com- ing? Everything goes on as it has since the Fathers died, as it has since it began at the creation." ⁵ They are choosing to forget that there were heav- ens at the beginning, and that the earth was formed by the word of God out of water and be- ⁶ tween the waters, ·so that the world of that time ⁷ was destroyed by being flooded by water. ·But by the same word, the present sky and earth are des- tined for fire, and are only being reserved until Judgment day so that all sinners may be destroyed.

⁸ But there is one thing, my friends, that you must never forget: that with the Lord, "a day" can mean a thousand years, and a thousand years ⁹ is like a day. ·The Lord is not being slow to carry out his promises, as anybody else might be called slow; but he is being patient with you all, wanting nobody to be lost and everybody to be brought ¹⁰ to change his ways. ·The Day of the Lord will come like a thief, and then with a roar the sky

will vanish, the elements will catch fire and fall apart, the earth and all that it contains will be burned up.

¹¹ Since everything is coming to an end like this, ¹² you should be living holy and saintly lives ·while you wait and long for the Day of God to come, when the sky will dissolve in flames and the elements melt in the heat. ·What we are waiting for ¹³ is what he promised: the new heavens and new earth, the place where righteousness will be at ¹⁴ home. ·So then, my friends, while you are waiting, do your best to live lives without spot or stain ¹⁵ so that he will find you at peace. ·Think of our Lord's patience as your opportunity to be saved: our brother Paul, who is so dear to us, told you this when he wrote to you with the wisdom that ¹⁶ is his special gift. ·He always writes like this when he deals with this sort of subject, and this makes some points in his letter hard to understand; these are the points that uneducated and unbalanced people distort, in the same way as they distort the ¹⁷ rest of scripture—a fatal thing for them to do. ·You have been warned about this, my friends; be careful not to get carried away by the errors of unprincipled people, from the firm ground that you ¹⁸ are standing on. ·Instead, go on growing in the grace and in the knowledge of our Lord and savior Jesus Christ. To him be glory, in time and in eternity. Amen.

☩

In reply to those who scoffed at the idea of a termination of the world that was to coincide with the return of Jesus Christ, our writer refers again to the Flood as the primary model for the Last Judgment. This time he makes a studied contrast of water and fire.

With the help of a mixture of Semitic theology and Greek cosmological speculation, he points out that the heaven and the earth are largely composed of water and owe their stability to water (3:5). Genesis 7 records that both the heavenly waters and the waters from the depths of the earth combined to destroy the world of Noah's time (2 P 3:6). According to intertestamental doctrine, the end of the world would be brought on not by water but by fire (3:10). And if there appears to be a delay in the ultimate conflagration, that is due to God's gracious patience, assures our writer (3:8–9).

Never losing sight of his moral perspective, the writer instructs his readers that the old will be replaced by a new creation. Inasmuch as goodness will characterize the new heaven and the new earth, it would be stupid to maintain a lifestyle that has no future (3:11–13).

In an echo of 1:5, the writer directs his addressees to make every effort to be the kind of people appropriate to the structure of the age to come (3:13). As St. Paul affirmed in Romans 2:4 God's patience aims to lead us to repentance.

Unfortunately, as the long history of biblical interpretation sadly attests, people will twist the Scriptures in support of interests that run counter to the divine purpose. St. Paul's writings are among the victims (see 2 P 2:18–19). Perhaps our writer's closing words (3:17–18) will help cut down the carnage.

STUDY QUESTIONS: It has been said: "Not fear of judgment but the character of the future gives shape to Christian moral and ethical integrity." Does this statement accurately reflect 2 Peter 3? Of what relevance is 2 Peter in a world that is accustomed to thinking of the earth in terms of an age of billions of years?

1 John
The First Letter of John

INTRODUCTION

A variety of literature in the New Testament is associated with the name of the Apostle John. It ranges from two letters of average length to a theological retelling of the story of Jesus Christ and a breathtaking scenario for the end of the world.

Since the early Church specialized in one doctrine, the Gospel, diversity of theological viewpoint was inevitable; for theology is the process of attempting to understand the meaning of the Gospel in terms of one's past and present experience and knowledge.

In the circle of believers who recognized the Apostle John as their principal spiritual ancestor, leaders emerged who felt a responsibility to share what they had learned through the process of tradition from him.

In response to fresh situations and problems the tradition would take on variations in theme and stress. But such topics as love, the importance of the Messiah's presence in the flesh, and eternal life as a present realization were dominant.

From only a brief acquaintance one can see that the three letters ascribed to John display a family relationship, and the slight variations in expression and perspective can be attributed to differences in geographical locale and local circumstances. The probability that they derive from two or even three different authors is itself a tribute to the harmony prevailing within the "Johannine" circle of congregations. Heresy begins at the point of distortion of the Gospel. Each of the three Letters of John aims to check any such process.

A rather interesting feature of the First Letter of John is the ellipse technique used by the writer. Instead of dividing his subject into defined parts for logical analysis, he develops his presentation with two foci in mind: Christian fellowship and the incarnate Messiah. No matter where we may happen to be in the document, we encounter these two themes. In essence they blend into one concept: PARTNERSHIP. Anyone who knows God in Jesus Christ is in partnership with anyone else who similarly knows God, and with profound ethical consequences.

The Second and Third Letters of John are of special interest because of their contrasting approach to the theme of HOSPITALITY, a topic that is closely related to the concerns expressed in the First Letter of John. The writer of Second John finds it necessary to discourage hospitality in some instances. Third John, on the other hand, describes a case of aweful inhospitality.

I invite you to share the stimulating thought world of these Three Letters of John. And I hope that you will help Christians face up to their unfortunate neglect of Third John especially.

1 John 1:1-4
THE THEME OF FELLOWSHIP

1 1 Something which has existed since the beginning,
that we have heard,
and we have seen with our own eyes;
that we have watched
and touched with our hands:
the Word, who is life—
this is our subject.
2 That life was made visible:
we saw it and we are giving our testimony,
telling you of eternal life
which was with the Father and has been made
visible to us.
3 What we have seen and heard
we are telling you
so that you too may be in union with us,
as we are in union
with the Father
and with his Son Jesus Christ.
4 We are writing this to you to make our own
joy complete.

✠

How to maintain cohesion of scattered Christians
became an increasingly perplexing problem as the
apostolic circle diminished and finally died out entirely.
The writer of First John therefore devotes an entire
essay to the topic: Fellowship of God's people.

If Christians were not to fall easy prey to ego-tripping teachers and administrators, it was necessary to establish lines of continuity with the main event: God's action in and with Jesus Christ. Insistence on the historical figure of Jesus was crucial if Christianity were not to degenerate into religious speculation or good views instead of good news.

To reinforce this point, the writer stresses the importance of personal contact with Jesus' Word and deed (1:1). Among the first guarantors of Jesus' identity are the apostles. In line after them are the people who received the traditions concerning Jesus Christ. Our writer evidently considers himself among the latter (1:2).

Fellowship derives its meaning and its pattern from the heavenly Parent-child relationship. Through association with Jesus Christ, the apostles and others who saw and heard him personally were privileged to share God's family circle. Others who wish to enter that fellowship must do so by responding affirmatively to the Christian message, which is transmitted by those who are already in the fellowship. Along this route of fidelity to the tradition Christian fellowship is broadened and its cohesion is strengthened (1:3). Each one can then say in concert with the cumulative family: "*We* have seen and heard" (1:1).

Unlike separatists and denominational exclusivists, the congregations that stand behind this communication affirm their apostolic witness (1:4).

1 John 1:5 – 2:11
NO COVER-UP

5   This is what we have heard from him,
and the message that we are announcing to
    you:
God is light; there is no darkness in him at all.
6   If we say that we are in union with God
while we are living in darkness,
we are lying because we are not living the
    truth.
7   But if we live our lives in the light,
as he is in the light,
we are in union with one another,
and the blood of Jesus, his Son,
purifies us from all sin.
8   If we say we have no sin in us,
we are deceiving ourselves
and refusing to admit the truth;
9   but if we acknowledge our sins,
then God who is faithful and just
will forgive our sins and purify us
from everything that is wrong.
10   To say that we have never sinned
is to call God a liar
and to show that his word is not in us.

2   1 I am writing this, my children,
to stop you sinning;
but if anyone should sin,
we have our advocate with the Father,
Jesus Christ, who is just;
2   he is the sacrifice that takes our sins away,
and not only ours,
but the whole world's.

3   We can be sure that we know God
     only by keeping his commandments.
4   Anyone who says, "I know him,"
     and does not keep his commandments,
     is a liar,
     refusing to admit the truth.
5   But when anyone does obey what he has said,
     God's love comes to perfection in him.
     We can be sure
     that we are in God
6   only when the one who claims to be living in
          him
     is living the same kind of life as Christ lived.
7   My dear people,
     this is not a new commandment that I am writ-
          ing to tell you,
     but an old commandment
     that you were given from the beginning,
     the original commandment which was the mes-
          sage brought to you.
8   Yet in another way, what I am writing to you,
     and what is being carried out in your lives as
          it was in his,
     is a new commandment;
     because the night is over
     and the real light is already shining.
9   Anyone who claims to be in the light
     but hates his brother
     is still in the dark.
10   But anyone who loves his brother is living in
          the light
     and need not be afraid of stumbling;
11   unlike the man who hates his brother and is
          in the darkness,
     not knowing where he is going,
     because it is too dark to see.

✠

1 John 1:5–7

To affirm a relationship with God means to accept
responsibility for moral and ethical responses that are

in harmony with such profession. Jewish writers call this the "way" of life or "walking" in God's commandments. Our writer adopts this terminology, which is validly rendered by JB as "living" the truth or "we live our lives" in the light. Deceptive outmaneuvering and exploitative domination, as detailed throughout the essay, constitute a "walk" (JB "living") in darkness (1:6).

God's purpose in permitting the death of the Son was to offer the world a fresh start and to re-establish communications. Life in the light is therefore the ongoing antidote to death in the darkness of sin (1:7).

1 John 1:8–10

Since the fellowship of God's people is the community of the forgiven, only those can enter it who are willing to face up to their sinfulness. Refusal to do so is self-deception and tantamount to vilification of the Deity. At the crucifixion of the Son, the immensity of humanity's guilt found projection against the dimensions of God's own magnanimity.

1 John 2:1–6

Through Jesus Christ God declares amnesty and pardon for the human race. Cover-up and pretentious piety are now obsolete (2:1–2). The Parent forgives and now says to the children, "Don't do it again."

God's love attains its objective when we honestly face up to the pattern of our sins and exchange them for one of loving actions. To be a child of God means that one is committed to love. Love is God's fundamental characteristic. And Jesus Christ exemplified it to the uttermost by living constantly with reference to the needs of others (2:3–6).

1 John 2:7–11

The essayist apologizes for repeating what the congregation already knows: God has acted significantly in their behalf through Jesus Christ. By implication, God's action is such that it involves the believers in extraordinarily new opportunity. From this perspective our writer's exhortation may be correctly termed a "new commandment" (2:7–8).

Since love has nothing to hide, it may be called walking in the light—that is, in openness and trust. Similarly, lovelessness corresponds to darkness, and it requires lies to cover its tracks (2:9–11).

STUDY QUESTIONS: How does the writer of 1 John justify the term "new commandment" in his rhetoric on love? How will application of his counsel on forgiveness assist in improving, for example, a strained marriage relationship?

1 John 2:12–29
TWO ARCHENEMIES

12 I am writing to you, my own children,
    whose sins have already been forgiven through
        his name;
13 I am writing to you, fathers,
    who have come to know the one
    who has existed since the beginning;
    I am writing to you, young men,
    who have already overcome the Evil One;
14 I have written to you, children,
    because you already know the Father;
    I have written to you, fathers,
    because you have come to know the one
    who has existed since the beginning;
    I have written to you, young men,
    because you are strong and God's word has
        made its home in you,
    and you have overcome the Evil One.
15 You must not love this passing world
    or anything that is in the world.
    The love of the Father cannot be
    in any man who loves the world,
16 because nothing the world has to offer
    —the sensual body,
    the lustful eye,
    pride in possessions—
    could ever come from the Father
    but only from the world;
17 and the world, with all it craves for,
    is coming to an end;
    but anyone who does the will of God
    remains for ever.

18   Children, these are the last days;
      you were told that an Antichrist must come,
      and now several antichrists have already ap-
          peared;
      we know from this that these are the last days.
19   Those rivals of Christ came out of our own
          number, but they had never really belonged;
      if they had belonged, they would have stayed
          with us;
      but they left us, to prove that not one of them
      ever belonged to us.
20   But you have been anointed by the Holy One,
      and have all received the knowledge.
21   It is not because you do not know the truth
          that I am writing to you
      but rather because you know it already
      and know that no lie can come from the truth.
22   The man who denies that Jesus is the Christ—
      he is the liar,
      he is Antichrist;
      and he is denying the Father as well as the
          Son,
23   because no one who has the Father can deny
          the Son,
      and to acknowledge the Son is to have the Fa-
          ther as well.
24   Keep alive in yourselves what you were taught
          in the beginning:
      as long as what you were taught in the begin-
          ning is alive in you,
      you will live in the Son
      and in the Father;
25   and what is promised to you by his own
          promise
      is eternal life.
26   This is all that I am writing to you about the
          people who are trying to lead you astray.
27   But you have not lost the anointing that he
          gave you,
      and you do not need anyone to teach you;
      the anointing he gave teaches you everything;
      you are anointed with truth, not with a lie,
      and as it has taught you, so you must stay in
          him.

28   Live in Christ, then, my children,
      so that if he appears, we may have full confi-
         dence,
      and not turn from him in shame
      at his coming.
29   You know that God is righteous—
      then you must recognize that everyone whose
         life is righteous
      has been begotten by him.

✠

1 John 2:12-17

In 2:12–14 our writer prepares his addressees for exposure of two lethal enemies: the WORLD and AN-TICHRIST.

Two pairs of three directives each compose the exhortation in 2:12–14. The "children" are the members of the Christian congregations addressed by the writer. They have known the exceptional love of the heavenly Parent, for they have received assurance of forgiveness (2:12).

Through repetition of his address to the "fathers" the writer reminds his auditors that fellowship is his main theme. The parents among them have a special responsibility for their children. Fortunately they are in a privileged position to offer appropriate guidance in obedient living. They have known the Son of God, and they themselves, being *God's* children, are well practiced in the art of partnership with the Parent of all parents (2:13–14).

Since young men ordinarily take pride in their strength and vigor, the writer compliments them for their victories over the "Evil One," the devil, who is no pushover. The Christian message has taken effect in

them as a continuing power for ethical decision
(2:13–14).

The tenses in verses 12–14 suggested past performance. But Christians cannot afford to let down their
guard, especially in the face of their most formidable
opponent: the WORLD (2:15–17).

"World" is the writer's comprehensive term for self-
gratification, instant satisfaction, manipulation of
others, and exploitative processes. In the lunge toward
recognition and success one may learn too late that the
forms and interests of the world, as well as the desire
for what it has to offer, are deceptively transient. An
"aching forehead and a parching tongue," as John
Keats warned, are the product of delights and pleasures
that lack a meaningful frame of reference. Performance
of the will of God alone ensures permanence.

1 John 2:18–29

The theme of rapid passage in verses 15–17 suggests
to the writer the topic of the last times. According to
opinion in various religious circles, an extraordinary
manifestation of evil called ANTICHRIST would take
place in the last stage of the world's existence (for example, see 2 Th 2). The writer thinks of the heretical
teachers in the circle of congregations under his care
and says that the expectation is evidently more than
fulfilled right in the bosom of the Christian fellowship.
Instead of one there are *many* (JB's "several" misses
the writer's irony). What further proof is needed that
time has almost run out? (2:18).

The fact that these heretics were once related to the
fellowship suggests some heart searching. Not everyone
claiming partnership with God is really a partner.
When all is said, these antichrists are deceivers, incapa-

ble of the honest and aboveboard relationships described earlier.

But how can conscientious Christians be sure that they will not fall into a similar classification? (2:19). Our writer approaches his answer to the question with a clever pun. The word "Christ" equals "Anointed One." Antichrists are therefore people in opposition to *the* Anointed One. *"But,"* implies our writer to his faithful adherents in the congregations, "you are *not* antichrists." On the contrary, "You have been anointed [*chrismed*] by the Holy One" (2:20).

Our writer's linkage of knowledge and anointing is significant. Apparently he views the anointing primarily as the Christian's understanding of the basic truth that God is the Parent of Jesus Christ and that we are brought into God's family through the Son, with a view to life that is in keeping with the divine purpose. Such understanding would be equivalent to the gift of the Holy Spirit, and where God is entrenched, the devil and his allies cannot enter.

A clearer definition of the heretics appears in verses 22–29. They deny that Jesus is the historical point of demonstration for God's great end-time action: the salvation of humanity (2:22). From clues in the Fourth Gospel and the two other Letters associated with the name of John it appears that these heretics are self-styled religious leaders who disavow dependence on tradition that claims the teaching of Jesus as ultimate authority. By denying that the Messiah has come in the flesh they endeavor to depreciate the value of instruction limited to the historical Jesus. Thereby they undercut esteemed teachers in the community and invite attention to their own speculations concerning God's intervention in human affairs.

These heretics are frequently classed as "gnostics," but this term suggests a more clearly defined type of

religious propagandists than the data warrant. It is in
fact as difficult to define gnosticism in the first century
as it is to summarize the belief patterns of all the de-
nominations that in our own day fall under the general
classification of "evangelical groups," which range
from one-congregation sects to communities numbering
six figures or more.

From our writer's perspective the false teachers are
menaces to the Christian community because of their
divisiveness. Their spirit of sectarianism is basically
one-upmanship, of the we-are-better-than-you type or
our-doctrine-is-more-pure-than-yours, with the implication we-sin-less-than-you-do.

In answer to such a divisive spirit, the writer emphasizes the good news that Jesus Christ is the Son of God,
who has come in the flesh. He is not saying that mere
assent or agreement with a formulation along these
lines constitutes salvation. Rather, in connection with
Jesus Christ as God's gift to humanity divine forgiveness finds dramatization. Denial of the Son's appearance in the flesh would therefore constitute a denial of God's beneficent self-disclosure.

Consent to the teaching that Jesus Christ really came
to our planet as a human being is in effect a confession
of sin and openness to our Parent's forgiveness. This
forgiveness is extended to all in the community who
share in such confession. They constitute the body of
believers, who are in partnership with God and with
one another (2:23–26).

The task of the teaching office in the Church is to
transmit unsullied this instruction concerning the fellowship that we have with one another through Jesus
Christ. Those who hold to or "stay" with this instruction (2:27) understand that forgiveness means possibility for a new life. They will be able to face Jesus
Christ without embarrassment *when* (not "if") he re-

turns. As 2:29 asserts, the genes will show. And the anointing of Jesus rubs off on the believers (2:27). The word play is patent. Far from being ANTI-Christ, they are superbly PRO-Christ.

STUDY QUESTIONS: In what forms did the "*me* decade" (John calls it "the world") meet you yesterday? What manifestations of *antichrist* have you encountered recently? What are some of the ways in which a practical denial of the incarnation is expressed today?

1 John 3:1–24
FUTURE-ORIENTED

1 **3** Think of the love that the Father has lavished
on us,
by letting us be called God's children;
and that is what we are.
Because the world refused to acknowledge
him,
therefore it does not acknowledge us.

2 My dear people, we are already the children
of God
but what we are to be in the future has not yet
been revealed;
all we know is, that when it is revealed
we shall be like him
because we shall see him as he really is.

3 Surely everyone who entertains this hope
must purify himself, must try to be as pure as
Christ.

4 Anyone who sins at all
breaks the law,
because to sin is to break the law.

5 Now you know that he appeared in order to
abolish sin,
and that in him there is no sin;

6 anyone who lives in God does not sin,
and anyone who sins
has never seen him or known him.

7 My children, do not let anyone lead you
astray:
to live a holy life
is to be holy just as he is holy;

8 to lead a sinful life is to belong to the devil,

since the devil was a sinner from the beginning.

It was to undo all that the devil has done
that the Son of God appeared.

9 No one who has been begotten by God sins;
because God's seed remains inside him,

he cannot sin when he has been begotten by
God.

10 In this way we distinguish the children of God
from the children of the devil:

anybody not living a holy life
and not loving his brother
is no child of God's.

11 This is the message
as you heard it from the beginning:
that we are to love one another;

12 not to be like Cain, who belonged to the Evil
One

and cut his brother's throat;

cut his brother's throat simply for this reason,
that his own life was evil and his brother lived
a good life.

13 You must not be surprised, brothers, when the
world hates you;

14 we have passed out of death and into life,
and of this we can be sure
because we love our brothers.

15 If you refuse to love, you must remain dead;
to hate your brother is to be a murderer,
and murderers, as you know, do not have eternal life in them.

16 This has taught us love—
that he gave up his life for us;

and we, too, ought to give up our lives for our
brothers.

17 If a man who was rich enough in this world's
goods

saw that one of his brothers was in need,
but closed his heart to him,

how could the love of God be living in him?

18 My children,
our love is not to be just words or mere talk,
but something real and active;

19   only by this can we be certain
      that we are children of the truth
      and be able to quiet our conscience in his
         presence,
20   whatever accusations it may raise against us,
      because God is greater than our conscience
         and he knows everything.
21   My dear people,
      if we cannot be condemned by our own con-
         science,
      we need not be afraid in God's presence,
22   and whatever we ask him,
      we shall receive,
      because we keep his commandments
      and live the kind of life that he wants.
23   His commandments are these:
      that we believe in the name of his Son Jesus
         Christ
      and that we love one another
      as he told us to.
24   Whoever keeps his commandments
      lives in God and God lives in him.
      We know that he lives in us
      by the Spirit that he has given us.

✠

1 John 3:1–3

The concluding summary of chapter 2 introduced
two ideas: (1) generation by God ("begotten by
him," 2:29); (2) Jesus' return (2:28). The writer now
uses these themes as a takeoff for further encouragement to new life.

Instruction concerning Jesus' return alerts us to the
future. But all of Christian living is future-oriented—
that is, the present is of a piece with the future, and the
future determines the nature of the present. Theologians call it "eschatological existence." In practice it is

openness to the surprising possibilities of innovative performance in behalf of other human beings.

As the children of God we have experienced the acme of parental love. Despite our sins God has taken us back into the family. Now we share God's basic characteristic—LOVE—as we relate lovingly to one another. This truth functions reciprocally with the other concerning the return of Jesus. For our writer this return is significant because of its moral and ethical implications. Jesus is the uniquely good human being. When he appears we shall see perfection itself, and we shall experience in ourselves the goodness that is his (3:3).

Far from being a drag, fullness of goodness is something to anticipate. The present is the training ground for the future. And in partnership with one another we begin to experience the future.

The rather abstract idea of innocence treated in 3:1–3 is now taken up in verses 4–12.

1 John 3:4–12

At first sight the writer seems to contradict statements made in 1:8–10, but the problem evaporates when we focus on the main thematic line: love of the brothers and sisters.

Sin is the opposite of love. Disruption of the partnership of believers, as perpetrated by the divisive tactics of the heretics, is sin or lawlessness (3:4). To be a child of God means commitment to the fellowship. Our writer understands this, of course, not in the sense of organizational security, but of careful concern for the well-being of others. When the writer says that such a person "cannot sin" (3:9) he is asserting that the person has sufficient resources for *not* sinning. False teachers cannot offer this assurance. Their exhortation

is without reference to the life and death of Jesus
Christ, whereby God demonstrates all willingness to
parent the believers. Such love begets love. "God's
seed" remains in the believer. The genes will show
(3:9).

What a contrast to the scene in Cain's city, Enoch-
ville, as described by the author of *Cain, Come Home!*

> The city is built on a foundation of desire and of fear.
> Its compensations for alienation make civilization possi-
> ble, but they do not touch the alienation itself. The fertile
> fields of boredom, self-pity, inequity, accusation, and con-
> flicting desire continue to breed violence. The sense of
> futility and of emptiness grows. Progress is repeatedly ex-
> posed as self-destruction. Wealth and freedom and pleas-
> ure bring only passing illusions of happiness. Youth fail
> to see purpose in what their parents are doing and yet
> cannot discover an alternative that would give them suf-
> ficient reason to live and to strive. The city is rocked with
> problems it ought to solve but cannot. Every escape that
> is tried yields only more futility and deeper disaster.

1 John 3:13–17

The story of Cain's fratricide (3:12) sets the stage
for the remarks in 3:13–17. *Love equals life* affirms
our writer, and he pairs this equation against *lack of
love equals death*. Paradoxically, however, love comes
to expression when one's own death is the ultimate gift
to another. Such is the case with the Son of God, whose
use of death spells possibility of life for all humanity.
Similarly when Christians permit their manipulative interests to die and begin to give themselves in the interests of others, life-productive love is in operation
(3:13–16).

The words "rich enough in this world's goods"
(3:17) express the thought that one has enough to
keep body and soul together. But what about those

who are unable to compete for necessities? God depends on the rest of the family to meet such needs (3:17).

1 John 3:18–24

The Gospel is indeed an invitation to an enterprising life. But what about conscientious Christians who might see a contradiction between what the writer said in 1:8–10 and what he affirmed in 3:9–10? What if they feel that their display of love is inadequate? (3:18–20). Our essayist offers words of consolation.

You can tell whether you are associated with the truth if you recognize that you are committed to genuine love (3:19). Your starting point is God's own loving forgiveness, spelled out in the life and death of the Son. This forgiveness is greater than any feelings of inadequacy you may experience as you encounter the need of responding within the fellowship (3:20). Encouraged by God's gracious contribution to your self-esteem, you can ask for further help in your display of love.

Remembrance of God's love in connection with the gift of Jesus Christ is the key to top-notch performance (3:21–23). And the Holy Spirit is the ultimate proof of Jesus' personal relationship to all who are in the Partnership (3:24).

STUDY QUESTION: What does 1 John mean by the affirmation that love equals life?

1 John 4:1–6
ANTICHRIST REVISITED

1 It is not every spirit, my dear people, that you
   can trust;
   test them, to see if they come from God;
   there are many false prophets, now, in the
   world.

2 You can tell the spirits that come from God
   by this:
   every spirit which acknowledges that Jesus the
   Christ has come in the flesh
   is from God;

3 but any spirit which will not say this of Jesus
   is not from God,
   but is the spirit of Antichrist,
   whose coming you were warned about.
   Well, now he is here, in the world.

4 Children,
   you have already overcome these false
   prophets,
   because you are from God and you have in
   you
   one who is greater than anyone in this world;

5 as for them, they are of the world,
   and so they speak the language of the world
   and the world listens to them.

6 But we are children of God,
   and those who know God listen to us;
   those who are not of God refuse to listen to us.
   This is how we can tell
   the spirit of truth from the spirit of falsehood.

✠

In the stylistic manner typical of the letter, the term "spirit" in 3:24 paves the way for a discourse on good and evil spirits (4:1).

Since God's own spirit is given to the believers (3:24), they have a criterion for determining the validity of what they hear from people who claim to be spokespersons for God. Once again the chief determinant is the message. Does the teacher emphasize the centrality of Jesus Christ—that is, the Gospel? The Gospel, the proclamation of God's ultimate expression of love, is *the* touchstone of orthodoxy (4:2).

The Gospel challenges our existence because it speaks of God as one who confronts us in our sinfulness and then greets us as our gracious forgiver. In contrast, false religious leaders appeal to our egos and in the name of religion suggest that God can be put in our debt. And they are all too ready to be the brokers (4:3–5).

With sharp insight into the responsibilities of his office, the Pope who succeeded Pius XII called himself *John* XXIII. Breathing the spirit of 1 John, he emphasized collegiality or partnership, with the Gospel as the moderator of the Church's mission to the world. Some few churchmen criticized him severely. They saw threats to their accustomed ways of doing religion.

It is indeed an easy matter to distinguish between the "spirit of truth" and the "spirit of falsehood" (4:6). The former directs one in the way of love. The latter causes one to stray from it. Truth fears no exposure. Falsehood majors in self-justification and specializes in making minority reports of the Church's experience dominant criteria of fellowship.

STUDY QUESTION: What is the best way to detect fraud
in religion? Try your answer out on
a number of religious claims you
have encountered in the media.

1 John 4:7 – 5:13
LOVE EQUALS KNOWLEDGE

7   My dear people,
    let us love one another
    since love comes from God
    and everyone who loves is begotten by God
        and knows God.
8   Anyone who fails to love can never have
        known God,
    because God is love.
9   God's love for us was revealed
    when God sent into the world his only Son
    so that we could have life through him;
10 this is the love I mean:
    not our love for God,
    but God's love for us when he sent his Son
    to be the sacrifice that takes our sins away.
11 My dear people,
    since God has loved us so much,
    we too should love one another.
12 No one has ever seen God;
    but as long as we love one another
    God will live in us
    and his love will be complete in us.
13 We can know that we are living in him
    and he is living in us
    because he lets us share his Spirit.
14 We ourselves saw and we testify
    that the Father sent his Son
    as savior of the world.
15 If anyone acknowledges that Jesus is the Son
        of God,
    God lives in him, and he in God.

16 We ourselves have known and put our faith in
God's love toward ourselves.
God is love
and anyone who lives in love lives in God,
and God lives in him.

17 Love will come to its perfection in us
when we can face the day of Judgment without fear;
because even in this world
we have become as he is.

18 In love there can be no fear,
but fear is driven out by perfect love:
because to fear is to expect punishment,
and anyone who is afraid is still imperfect in
love.

19 We are to love, then,
because he loved us first.

20 Anyone who says, "I love God,"
and hates his brother,
is a liar,
since a man who does not love the brother that
he can see
cannot love God, whom he has never seen.

21 So this is the commandment that he has given
us,
that anyone who loves God must also love his
brother.

5 1 Whoever believes that Jesus is the Christ
has been begotten by God;
and whoever loves the Father that begot him
loves the child whom he begets.

2 We can be sure that we love God's children
if we love God himself and do what he has
commanded us;

3 this is what loving God is—
keeping his commandments;

4 and his commandments are not difficult,
because anyone who has been begotten by
God
has already overcome the world;
this is the victory over the world—
our faith.

5 Who can overcome the world?

Only the man who believes that Jesus is the
Son of God:

6 Jesus Christ who came by water and blood,
not with water only,
but with water and blood;
with the Spirit as another witness—
since the Spirit is the truth—

7 so that there are three witnesses,

8 the Spirit, the water and the blood,
and all three of them agree.

9 We accept the testimony of human witnesses,
but God's testimony is much greater,
and this is God's testimony,
given as evidence for his Son.

10 Everybody who believes in the Son of God
has this testimony inside him;
and anyone who will not believe God
is making God out to be a liar,
because he has not trusted
the testimony God has given about his Son.

11 This is the testimony:
God has given us eternal life
and this life is in his Son;

12 anyone who has the Son has life,
anyone who does not have the Son does not
have life.

13 I have written all this to you
so that you who believe in the name of the
Son of God
may be sure that you have eternal life.

✠

1 John 4:7–16

Typical of his style, the writer expands on the theme
of knowledge with which he terminated 4:1–6.

Philosophers and theologians long have catalogued
and described the divine attributes. Atheist Madalyn
O'Hair knows how to refute all the standard arguments
used to affirm the existence of God. Our writer does

not fall into the trap. For him the doctrine of the Gospel is not grist for intellectual exercise. Nor is the fellowship of Christians a debating society. When believers engage in what they are best equipped to do—partnering in love—God becomes easily demonstrable (4:7–8).

It now becomes even clearer why our writer has stressed the importance of affirming the Son's appearance in human history. It was a foregone conclusion that the world, with its own ideas on how to handle God, would reject this intrusion of the Almighty into its affairs. But God would not be rebuffed. Through the gift of Jesus God shows extraordinary capacity for canceling sin and even clears humanity of the most horrendous crime in all the annals of the universe: the rejection of the Son of God! (4:9–10).

In bafflement before such love, our writer now pens one of the most amazing sentences in all literature (4:11). One might have expected him to say that we in turn ought to love God, but the expectation is misplaced. Given his attack on the *quid-pro-quo*, grease-my-palm-and-I'll-grease-yours approach, it is not surprising that he shows God diverting our response to the heavenly Parent in the direction of our fellow human beings. God loves others through *us*. It is out of the question for anyone even to suggest: Now they owe us (4:12).

Love is the main gene, and we are carriers of the divine character. Put another way, when we love we give proof that we have received the Spirit (4:13). This Spirit is not some mysterious cosmic force. Nor is it a congeries of exotic gifts to incite divisions in the partnership of faith. God shares the Spirit, and love is the badge of divine identity (4:13–16).

At first reading, the rhetoric about love of the brothers and sisters may seem protective and without

responsibility to the surrounding culture. A closer look
suggests uncommon insight. Casual relationships make
few demands. It is easier to be polite to relative
strangers than to members of one's own family. The
frequency with which ecclesiastical infighting makes the
front page is a grotesque scandal. If Churches are to
maintain credibility as they proclaim a message of salvation for all the world (4:14), they must show more
expert use within their ranks of the Gospel's principal
product—love. There is no better practice ground than
the immediate fellowship.

1 John 4:17 – 5:13

In 4:17–18 our writer expands on the theme of love.
As pointed out earlier (3:1–3), the writer's conception
of the future is moral dynamism. The future will be in
continuity with the present. Since love is the standard
of eternal life, those who now specialize in it can face
the day of judgment with complete confidence. This
pride-in-the-job motif is in striking contrast to the mor-
bid anxiety with which many Christians have been
taught to approach Judgment Day.

Love continues to be the theme of 4:19 – 5:4, but
with ever stronger emphasis on divine priority. God's
love is prior to any that we can display, and it shows itself in order to put us in touch with our fellow human
beings (4:19). God is not impressed with love in the
abstract. Love for the Deity is concretized as we display love for those whom God loves.

Since Jesus is the focal point of God's loving demonstration, belief in Christ is both a confession of sin and
grateful acceptance of the pardon that God offers
through him. Such response to God identifies one as a
child of God and opens one to loving relationships with
the rest of the family (5:1–2).

To love the other means to overcome the temptation of the world to exploit and manipulate for self-interest. And it is God, the loving Parent, who exhorts us to achieve that victory. As children we welcome the opportunity to carry out our Parent's directions, all of which aim to dedicate us to the best interests of humanity. Our faith in God's action in Jesus commits us to victorious achievement of that objective (5:3–4).

The terms "faith" and "victory" in 5:4 lead the writer into his crescendo in 5:5–13 on the importance of the Jesus of history. In an echo of the Fourth Gospel, where Jesus is described as attested by water and blood (Jn 19:34), the writer draws attention to Jesus' humanity (1 Jn 5:6–8).

According to Semitic thought both water and blood suggest life, but blood also connotes death. The mystery of Jesus' person is that he uniquely combines the experience of life and death, and this combination is God's instrument to move the believers from death to life. For this reason belief in Jesus Christ as one who shared our humanity is fundamental. In connection with him, God's power to change a person from deathways to lifeways finds display (5:5–6).

The Spirit attests the truth of God's action in Jesus Christ. The function of Jesus is not to provide data for dogmatic debate. Divine self-validation takes place in Christians through the faith that God creates in Jesus Christ, who is the supreme evidence and exposition of divine love (5:6–9). In connection with the Son's death and resurrection God attests that we have eternal life (5:10–12). And this life is, as the writer has repeatedly affirmed, a partnership in love.

STUDY QUESTION: How does 1 John's view of the future affect his ethical thinking?

1 John 5:14–21
NO AFTERTHOUGHTS

14 We are quite confident that if we ask him for
      anything,
    and it is in accordance with his will,
    he will hear us;
15 and, knowing that whatever we may ask, he
      hears us,
    we know that we have already been granted
      what we asked of him.
16 If anybody sees his brother commit a sin
    that is not a deadly sin,
    he has only to pray, and God will give life to
      the sinner
    —not those who commit a deadly sin;
    for there is a sin that is death,
    and I will not say that you must pray about
      that.
17 Every kind of wrongdoing is sin,
    but not all sin is deadly.
18 We know that anyone who has been begotten
      by God
    does not sin,
    because the begotten Son of God protects him,
    and the Evil One does not touch him.
19 We know that we belong to God,
    but the whole world lies in the power of the
      Evil One.
20 We know, too, that the Son of God has come,
    and has given us the power
    to know the true God.
    We are in the true God,
    as we are in his Son, Jesus Christ.

This is the true God,
this is eternal life.

21   Children, be on your guard against false gods.

⊹

The gift of eternal life is, as 5:13 climactically
affirmed, the acme of divine philanthropy. But there is
more. Believers can come to this generous Parent with
any request that has to do with the carrying out of
God's will (5:14–15).

At first sight verses 14–15 appear to be after-
thoughts. But their connection with the rest of the
essay is eminently clear when we understand that a
besetting problem among Christians is the tendency to
consider oneself better than the other. On the contrary,
urges the writer, we are to seek the other's improvement. To that end we are to undergird our positive ex-
pressions of love with prayer in behalf of our brothers
and sisters that God would forgive them and help them
to experience life in its fullness (5:16). Such prayer
implies attitudes of patience and understanding.
Thereby the community mounts guard against zealots
who insist on affirming that they are purer than the
rest.

In connection with his plea for patience our writer
makes a statement that has made some Christians
scratch their heads. What in the world is a "deadly
sin"? And why is it to be deleted from one's prayer
list?

It is first of all important to note that our writer does
not use our rhetoric of "forgiveness," which usually
means: "Never mind, forget it." His diction rather con-
veys the thought of granting a pardon, with a view to
reinstatement. Second, he is conscious of a contrast between conduct that now and then misses the objectives

of partnership in the Gospel and the mindset that is inimical to the very concept of such partnership. In the first instance we deal openly with the offenders if their sins are serious enough to merit rebuke. If they accept the rebuke we can assure them that God pardons them, and the community's prayer for God's pardon assures them that their fellowship with the rest remains intact. In the writer's rhetoric this assurance is equivalent to "life" (5:16).

In most cases of interpersonal problems it will be sufficient simply to ask God to pardon the other, and that will be a prophylactic against resentment and hostility. But there are sins that cannot be pardoned, in the sense that business can go on as usual.

God's general announcement of pardon at the cross is valid. But, as the writer has repeatedly asserted, that pardon is at the same time a gracious invitation to share the divine fellowship and to partner in love with one another. Refusal to engage in that partnership is a determination to opt for death instead of life. And the symptoms of such death are very real. As described in 2:15–19, they include preoccupation with ego interests, a spirit of isolationism that seduces others into distortions of the Gospel, and a separatistic arrogance whose misdirected sense of alleged purer models of belief precludes the very idea of repentance. And without repentance there can be no pardon.

This is not to say that God will not be able to break through the hard crust. But Christians concerned about the larger partnership in the Gospel will have to say: "We are sorry, and we hold no ill will. In that sense we forgive you. But you yourselves are closing the door to any meaningful relationship either with us or with God. Since you are obviously not interested in a pardon, it would be ridiculous of us to ask God to pardon you." Love is obviously not synonymous with sentimentality.

The fact that we are to pray for one another means that the community operates in a pardoning capacity. In this respect believers function as God's children, whose chief characteristic is love in the face of sinfulness. Yet it is true that a child of God "does not sin" (5:18). This is the paradox: children of God, yet prone to errors. But they are no longer to be termed SINNERS. Our writer's careful use of tenses displays a fine awareness of the principle: Put down the action, not the person! Throughout his essay our author has helped his readers cultivate a high level of self-esteem. Here he gives it a final undergirding.

Jesus Christ, God's unique offspring, keeps all God's other offspring under guard. He will not permit the "Evil One" to claim them as his prey (5:18–19). This protective policy preserves God's children in their weakness, and this is why it can be said that they "cannot sin" (3:9). Sinning is no longer our lifestyle. God's Son gives us insight into the truth. This means we are able to distinguish between what is prejudicial to life and what is in harmony with it. And love overcomes all.

Ultimately the Son is the point at which the meaning of God in his fullness emerges. Any theology that depreciates God's interest in making contact with our fragile existence is anti-Christian.

Apart from Jesus Christ eternal life has no significance (5:20). This affirmation is not a theoretical identification, but a dynamic exhortation. Therefore the document terminates with the admonition: Keep yourself from idolatry (5:21). Of course, this means to be on your guard against the kind of teaching proposed by the heretics. Idolatry is notoriously divisive. Anything that leads away from love for the brother and sister is therefore tantamount to idolatry.

STUDY QUESTIONS: How does 1 John protect you against anxiety over some of the failure you may experience in dealing with other people's weaknesses? In what ways is the instruction of 1 John conducive to good mental health?

2 *John*
The Second Letter of John

INTRODUCTION

Of the two very brief documents traditionally ascribed to John, the one known as Third John is closest in form and style to ancient everyday letters. In the Second Letter of John the writer is conscious of a broader audience and adapts the more normal one-to-one communication to the situation. The result is a slightly more official tone in his letter, but without the heavier magisterial chancery beat of a Pauline epistle.

The writer's primary concern is that the recipients do not fall victims to promoters of doctrinal novelties that tamper with the basic connection between the person of Jesus Christ and the moral and social integrity of the congregation.

2 John 1–6
THE ELDER AND THE LADY

1   From the Elder: my greetings to the Lady, the
    chosen one, and to her children, she whom I love
    in the truth—and I am not the only one, for so do
2   all who have come to know the truth—because
    of the truth that lives in us and will be with us for
3   ever. ·In our life of truth and love, we shall have
    grace, mercy and peace from God the Father and
    from Jesus Christ, the Son of the Father.
4   It has given me great joy to find that your chil-
    dren have been living the life of truth as we were
5   commanded by the Father. ·I am writing now,
    dear lady, not to give you any new command-
    ment, but the one which we were given at the be-
    ginning, and to plead: let us love one another.
6   To love is to live according to his command-
    ments: this is the commandment which you have
    heard since the beginning, to live a life of love.

✠

Our writer calls himself simply "the Elder" (verse
1). This churchman evidently had jurisdiction of sorts
over at least two groups of congregations located in
separate metropolitan areas. Since the name of the recipients' town would be written on the outside of the
letter after it had been rolled up and sealed, it was not
necessary for the Elder to specify the locale of the
"Lady" (verse 1), his term for the receiving congre-

gation. The recipients would of course know who the Elder or Presbyter was, as well as the locale of the "Sister" mentioned in verse 13. The bearer of the letter (usually a friend, not a government employee, as in our time) would be able to answer queries concerning the contents.

In the absence of any clue to the location either of the sender or the receivers, we shall in the interests of clarity arbitrarily assign the ancient city of Hieropolis to the writer and Seleucia to his addressees.

Christians near the end of the first century were a tiny minority and naturally had to meet in private homes. A dozen people, give or take a few, would ordinarily constitute a congregation. St. Paul's letter to Philemon is but one piece of evidence for a widespread practice.

The first group to meet in Seleucia would be the founding congregation in that town and its environs. Being a resourceful minority they would in a short time develop an efficient communications network. Responsibility for supervision of all the house churches would be assumed by a person recognized for wisdom and understanding. Both Jewish and secular society furnished the title: *Elder*.

All the Christians in Seleucia would be known collectively as "the Church in Seleucia." But the founding house church (in our writer's terminology, "Chosen Lady") would be the most natural recipient of a communication from another locality. Through this central house church it would go to the others in Seleucia (the Lady's "children"). As at Seleucia, Hieropolis has a "chosen" lady and her "children" (verse 13).

Since both founding churches are called sisters, they may be the product of missionary activity carried on by an unmentioned third party. Apparently our writer was a member of either the founding church in Hieropolis,

or of one of its related house churches. He may have
been appointed by the Apostle John himself to serve as
liaison official for the Christians in Hieropolis and
Seleucia. To avoid a dictatorial tone the Elder adopts
the warmth of a one-to-one communication in a document for which he has numerous auditors in mind.
Hence the singular term "Lady" (verse 1) easily gives
way to plural modes of address, as in verses 6, 10, and
12, where the word "you" might well be rendered "you
people."

KNOW YOUR DIGNITY

Charlatans of many pious varieties preyed on people's religious interests. The Elder therefore emphasizes that his concern is genuine and is shared by all
who, like him, know "the truth" (verse 1). This means
they act on the principle that a vertical relationship
with God is to be matched by responsible acceptance
of a horizontal relationship with their peers.

Since the fellowship of Christians transcends socia-
bility, the Elder affirms that he and all other true
Christians "love" the "chosen" lady and her associates.
And they do this not out of ulterior motives or poten-
tial material reciprocity, but simply because the truth
has linked them all together (verse 1).

But will it last? The Elder assures it, with emphasis.
God is the Parent, first of all of Jesus Christ, who is the
Son par excellence, and then of all the believers. They
can be certain of God's abiding generosity ("grace"),
sensitivity to need ("mercy"), and goodwill ("peace").
God acts with an openness that elicits trust and approaches humanity with genuine affection and concern.
When this outreach is reciprocated, the total family—
the Parent, the Son, and the believers—enjoy a unique
relationship (verses 2–3).

Aware of the many phony displays of affection in

the world, the Elder rings further changes on the theme
of genuineness. Every culture has its own distinctive
patterns either for keeping its guard up or for exploit-
ing those who let their guard down. To reverse the
trend our writer urges all the members to develop the
lifestyle of an open community, in keeping with the
founding principle of genuine affection. All the instructions of Jesus give expression to this basic objective:
Seek the best interests of the other (verses 4–6). Said
Leo the Great, "Christian, know your dignity."

STUDY QUESTIONS: Would 2 John say that the unity of
the Church is to be *achieved?* Or
would he say that it is to be *maintained?* What is the difference from
his point of view?

2 John 7–11
BEWARE OF IMPOSTERS

7 There are many deceivers about in the world, refusing to admit that Jesus Christ has come in the flesh. They are the Deceiver; they are the
8 Antichrist. ·Watch yourselves, or all our work
9 will be lost and not get the reward it deserves. ·If anybody does not keep within the teaching of Christ but goes beyond it, he cannot have God with him: only those who keep to what he taught
10 can have the Father and the Son with them. ·If anyone comes to you bringing a different doctrine, you must not receive him in your house or
11 even give him a greeting. ·To greet him would make you a partner in his wicked work.

✠

From the Elder's perspective the Church has only one doctrine—the GOSPEL. All instruction in the Christian community ultimately derives from it. And the Elder and most of his recipients are in accord with this unanimous apostolic tradition. Some, however, are deviating from the truth and refuse to admit that Jesus Christ actually made his appearance as a real human being. For such rebels the Elder reserves the term of ultimate personification of evil—ANTICHRIST (verse 7).

What in the world is so serious about denying that

the Messiah made his appearance in the person of the historical Jesus? An attack on two main lines of error in this doctrinal aberration surfaces in the Elder's discussion:

1. The deviants apparently presuppose that the Deity and matter are mutually incompatible. Such a view guts the Christian message (verse 8). The depths of divine involvement with the world and God's method of coping with sin find demonstration precisely in connection with the life and experiences of Jesus.

2. The errorists make an elitist appeal. In place of quality of love they make transmission of a body of esoteric knowledge the goal of revelation. This approach isolates the less intellectual, generates divisions, and destroys the fundamental aim and function of the Gospel: to extend the fellowship of the Parent and the Son to the members of the believing community so that they might be able to relate in love to one another (verses 9-10).

One doctrine—namely, the teaching that God has acted uniquely in the Jesus of history to solve the problem of humanity's vertical relationship—nourishes the horizontal oneness of the community. Anyone who deviates from it is to be denied hospitality (verse 10). Since greetings in the Mediterranean world were far less casual than most of ours and might even open the door to debate on religious and theological matters, the Elder advises against them when encountering errorists (verses 10-11).

2 John 12–13
HOPE TO SEE YOU SOON

12   There are several things I have to tell you, but
      I have thought it best not to trust them to paper
      and ink. I hope instead to visit you and talk to you
      personally, so that our joy may be complete.
13   Greetings to you from the children of your sis-
      ter, the chosen one.

☩

From the personal touch in verse 12 it is easy to understand why modern readers have so many question
marks over passages in biblical epistles. The writers either expected their dispatchers to fill in orally whatever
information was necessary or, as in this case, they anticipated personal exchange of mutual concerns.

To the end the Elder carries out the theme of
UNITY OF THE FELLOWSHIP. His joy is at its
peak in personal encounter. And he shares with the recipients the warm interest of all the Christians in the
locality from which he is writing (verses 12–13).

STUDY QUESTIONS: In the light of 2 John what is the
                  fundamental reason for the hostility
                  frequently displayed between mem-
                  bers of one denomination toward
                  those of another? What solutions
                  does he offer?

3 John
The Third Letter of John

INTRODUCTION

Congregations of Christians in the first century were not large, but there would be numerous clusters, especially in metropolitan areas (see the comment on 2 Jn 1–6). Each cluster would have at least one leader or presbyter (elder). From the Pastoral Epistles (1 Tm, 2 Tm, and Tt) we may conclude that it was not uncommon to link a number of clusters with one another through an elder. Some arrangement of this kind seems to be suggested by Third John, for the elder-writer is not welcome in the cluster or group of clusters under Diotrephes' immediate supervision. As the writer puts it: "He likes to put himself first."

This document is one of the most neglected pieces in the New Testament. Yet its message is of prime importance. Ego-tripping, personality cultism, and isolationism on the grounds of superior understanding of the truth are perennial hazards to the integrity of the Church.

3 John 1–8
GAIUS—GOOD EXAMPLE

1 From the Elder: greetings to my dear friend
2 Gaius, whom I love in the truth. ·My dear friend,
I hope everything is going happily with you and
that you are as well physically as you are spiritu-
3 ally. ·It was a great joy to me when some brothers
came and told of your faithfulness to the truth,
4 and of your life in the truth. ·It is always my
greatest joy to hear that my children are living according to the truth.

5 My friend, you have done faithful work in
looking after these brothers, even though they
6 were complete strangers to you. ·They are a proof
to the whole Church of your charity and it would
be a very good thing if you could help them on
their journey in a way that God would approve.
7 It was entirely for the sake of the name that they
set out, without depending on the pagans for any-
8 thing; ·it is our duty to welcome men of this sort
and contribute our share to their work for the
truth.

✠

A secular letter written by a non-Christian in the
second century begins as follows:

From Serapis: heartfelt greetings to her children
Ptolemaeus, Apolinaria, and Ptolemaeus. Above all I pray
that this letter finds you well, for nothing is more im-

portant to us. I bow before my Lord Serapis and pray that I may receive word that you are in good health, even as I pray for your general welfare. . . . I rejoiced when I received letters informing me that you were well recovered.

In his letter to Gaius the writer similarly begins with a reference to physical health (verse 2) but then moves on to speak of Gaius' spiritual well-being (verses 3–4).

The Elder is delighted with Gaius because he practices his religion (verse 4). Such integrity of avowed claim and performance was highly prized also outside the Christian tradition. Thousands of inscriptions from antiquity attest to public recognition of officials and ordinary citizens for exhibiting extraordinary character.

Gaius receives a special accolade for his hospitality to itinerant missionaries (verse 5). Unlike some contemporary philosophers and priests who made their livelihood by begging from anyone whom they met, these emissaries of the Gospel were dependent solely on the contributions and hospitality of their fellow believers (verse 7). That such a support system was considered vital to the prestige and freedom of the Gospel is apparent from the words of Jesus preserved in Mark 6:8–10, Matthew 10:9, and Luke 9:3.

By providing for the sustenance of the Lord's agents, Christians share in the enterprise of proclaiming the truth—the message of salvation (verse 8). By taking no money from non-Christians they declare that the message is God's GIFT to the world.

3 John 9–10
DIOTREPHES—BAD EXAMPLE

9   I have written a note for the members of the church, but Diotrephes, who seems to enjoy being
10 in charge of it, refuses to accept us. ·So if I come, I shall tell everyone how he has behaved, and about the wicked accusations he has been circulating against us. As if that were not enough, he not only refuses to welcome our brothers, but prevents the other people who would have liked to from doing it, and expels them from the church.

✠

Apparently the Elder has tried to communicate with the congregation of which Gaius appears to be a member, but without success. Diotrephes, otherwise lost to history, is a personality cultist and refuses to recognize the spiritual contributions that the Elder might make to the congregation where Diotrephes is in control. Not only that, he discourages people who show hospitality to the traveling missionaries (verses 9–10).

Like the long line of denominational exclusivists after him, he was clearly saying to the rest of Christendom: "NO TRESPASSING!" Not that he lacked reasons. It was one way to keep his church pure and free from the possibility of false teaching. Had not the Lord and the apostles issued numerous warnings on the subject? (For example, see Mk 13:6; Ac 20:20–31; Rm 16:17–18.)

3 John 11–15
DEMETRIUS—GOOD EXAMPLE

11 My dear friend, never follow such a bad example, but keep following the good one; anyone who does what is right is a child of God, but the person who does what is wrong has never seen God.

12 Demetrius has been approved by everyone, and indeed by the truth itself. We too will vouch for him and you know that our testimony is true.

13 There were several things I had to tell you but I would rather not trust them to pen and ink.

14 However, I hope to see you soon and talk to you

15 personally. ·Peace be with you; greetings from your friends; greet each of our friends by name.

✠

Notes of recommendation were common in antiquity. Romans 16:1–2 advertises the merits of Phoebe. Here an otherwise obscure Demetrius breaks into history.

Demetrius may have had a position similar to the one held by Diotrephes, but in a different locality. Unlike Diotrephes he enjoys the respect and appreciation of the entire Christian community. Nor is the adulation misplaced. Demetrius does not function behind a façade of political manipulation. His performance springs out of genuine concern for God and for people (verse 12). Such unalloyed behavior is called, in contrast to deceptive diplomacy, "living according to the truth" (verse 4).

The Elder then contributes his own testimony concerning Demetrius' character. Gaius can count on it, for the Elder is not in the habit of talking out of both sides of his mouth. What he says is what he means! (verse 12).

Verses 13–15 find echoes in correspondence of every culture. There are some things that are better left to discussion under four eyes.

STUDY QUESTIONS: What contributions does 3 John make to the improvement of collegiality on the part of leaders in Christendom today? How might unofficial Christians take the lead in promoting the real unity of the fellowship of believers?

The Letter of Jude

INTRODUCTION

Among the liveliest and most challenging pieces of rhetoric in the New Testament is the brief tract known as the Letter of Jude. Yet we know little about its author, less about the recipients, and can only guess at the reason for its composition.

Although the language of the greeting points rather conclusively to Jude the brother of the Lord (see Mk 6:3; Mt 13:55), we are still faced with two probabilities. Either this Jude himself wrote the document, or a later Christian leader used Jude's name to encourage interest in his own communication. The apparent lateness of the document, including especially the manner in which the early apostolic age is presented, favors pseudonymous authorship of what is really a tract in letter form.

From the polemical tone of the document it appears that a power struggle was going on in the circle of congregations addressed by the writer. The taproot of the problem can be traced to Jerusalem.

For some years James the brother of the Lord had been an influential Jewish-Christian leader in Jerusalem. Quite probably after his death in the year 62 his brother Jude moved into prominence. The fall of Jerusalem in the year 70 was extremely traumatic for the Jewish wing of the Church. Important traditional sources of stability were in danger of extinction, and others had been obliterated. Add to this the earlier success of the Gentile mission, and it is not difficult to assess the real and imagined peril.

Under the influence of Greco-Roman thought patterns, articulate members of the Christian community would introduce what the more Jewishly and traditionally oriented would interpret as speculative theology. "Gnosticism" is the umbrella term for some forms of this type of thought. More liberated Christians, on the other hand, would tend to be wary of control by a coterie of extreme traditionalists from either Jewish or Gentile background or both.

With his invocation of apostolic tradition as a unifying force, the writer hoped to defuse an explosive situation. By issuing the tract under Jude's name, but with the evident submergence of his own authority under that of apostolic tradition, he intended to allay fears of domination by the Jewishly oriented wing. At the same time he aimed to alert his congregations to the hazards of a movement without deep roots in Jewish tradition.

To sharpen his point the author used diction that invites some discount from a modern reader. As in the sociopolitical sphere, the "other side" in religious controversy ordinarily bears the brunt of what are known in political circles as buzz words. In an election year charges of "dirty tricks" are especially rampant. Corporations make "obscene profits." But no one seriously thinks that all politicians are guilty of the variety of deeds committed by participants in President Nixon's Watergate caper. Nor would anyone conclude that General Motors engages in what is literally known as prostitution. Such terms are evidently used to convey a sense of moral outrage over exploitation of the powerless and insensitivity to their needs. Similarly Jude's targets appear at the surface level of language to be card carriers of an ecclesiastical syndicate.

It is well therefore to remember that to a Jewishly oriented mind any departure from centuries-old tradition might mean a headlong plunge into moral disaster. The writer's negative description is in effect, then, a rhetorical caricature, a verbal cartoon. In ancient times the device was a standard feature of a form of communication known as DIATRIBE, the stock in trade of the street preachers in the Greco-Roman world.

That some of the epithets might have applied without discount is probable. There will always be those who are prepared to stretch the possibilities of a new idea to the very limits of absurdity. And sexual deviations are not seldom associated with pathological promotion of religious cult. On the other hand, it is a besetting sin of polemicists to make the crimes of a minority the common denominator for a broad range of positions that they oppose.

Writing in the second century, a bishop named Irenaeus specialized in heresy hunting and concentrated on hedonistic and libertinistic features in some gnostic enclaves. Fortunately we now possess a number of books written by early gnostics, and their authors in the main appear to have been earnest seekers with higher than average moral and ethical standards.

In the commentary proper the name Jude will serve as surrogate for the writer, whoever he may have been.

STUDY QUESTIONS: How do contemporary attitudes and practices relating to the rights and obligations of authors and publishers compare with ancient practices as sketched in the Introduction? In what ways do the introductory data on Jude modify, if at all, your previous understanding of the Letter?

Jude 1–2
GREETINGS FROM A SLAVE

1 From Jude, servant of Jesus Christ and brother
   of James; to those who are called, to those who
   are dear to God the Father and kept safe for Jesus
2 Christ, ·wishing you all mercy and peace and love. ·

✠

Jude takes a no-nonsense approach with the very
first words of his letter. He might have pulled rank and
identified himself as "brother of Jesus Christ and
James." Instead he lets his hearers know what constitutes chain of command and seniority in the Church.

By calling himself the SLAVE (translated "servant"
in JB and most versions) of Jesus Christ he affirms that
the latter is his Lord and MASTER. Any prestige that
might derive from Jude's relationship to his brother
James is ultimately secondary to the fundamental allegiance that ALL Christians must share.

Standing alone, the master-slave model would offer
little attraction. Jude is quick therefore to display the
prestigious identity of his addressees. Far from being
menials, they are like guests who have been invited to
share in great expectations. God, who is the Parent of
their Master, is also the Parent who is committed in
love to the Christian community. Slaves we are, yet

brothers and sisters, along with Jude and James, in the
family of God.

In the body of the letter Jude will write about security measures that must be taken against the counter-
revolutionaries. Here he assures his addressees that
God is keeping them safe for Jesus Christ.

Jude 3–7
CASE HISTORIES OF LOSERS

³ My dear friends, at a time when I was eagerly looking forward to writing to you about the salvation that we all share, I have been forced to write to you now and appeal to you to fight hard for the faith which has been once and for all en-
⁴ trusted to the saints. ·Certain people have infiltrated among you, and they are the ones you had a warning about, in writing, long ago, when they were condemned for denying all religion, turning the grace of our God into immorality, and rejecting our only Master and Lord, Jesus Christ.
⁵ I should like to remind you—though you have already learned it once and for all—how the Lord rescued the nation from Egypt, but afterward he still destroyed the men who did not trust him.
⁶ Next let me remind you of the angels who had supreme authority but did not keep it and left their appointed sphere; he has kept them down in the dark, in spiritual chains, to be judged on the
⁷ great day. ·The fornication of Sodom and Gomorrah and the other nearby towns was equally unnatural, and it is a warning to us that they are paying for their crimes in eternal fire.

✠

In typical Jewish fashion Jude views the end of world history as the ultimate experience of salvation for God's people. At that time God will release the

believers from everything that prevents realization of
all the benefits and objectives God has in mind for
them as persons. So attractive is the subject that Jude
would have liked to have used all his papyrus on this
positive theme. But counterrevolutionary forces who
are undermining the integrity of the Christian community call for a change in plan.

Claiming to acknowledge Jesus Christ as Lord and
Master, they have private agendas to which they render
prior allegiance. The writer of 1 Timothy 6:2 hints at
slaves who take advantage of kind masters. In the exaggerated street rhetoric of his time our author lets us
know that these people are worse. They turn grace into
an excuse for going on a spree of sin (verse 4). In the
face of their attack on the integrity of the community
Jude urges his addressees to contest all the more
strongly for fidelity to their first commitment (verse 3).

A curious feature of the three recipients of divine
judgment cited in verses 5–7 is the close initial contact
they had with the Deity.

On the Israelites' march out of Egypt God's presence was apparent in the pillar of cloud that led them
by day and the pillar of fire that gave them light at
night (see Ex 14–15). Then, on the threshold of entry
into the promised land, they were consigned to forty
years of wandering in the wilderness (see Nb 14). Reason? They failed to recognize the moral dimension of
faith (see Ps 95; 1 Co 10). Jude's point? They weren't
as close to the end of time as we are, and look at what
happened to them! (verse 5).

For his second example of punished insurgence Jude
(verse 6) dips into an apocalyptic work popular in his
time. Known as the *Book of Enoch*, this bizarre story
of rebellion in celestial headquarters captivated many
of Jude's contemporaries who looked for a radical solution to what they considered the impossible mess of

history. God would finally call a halt. Good would triumph. And evil would be forever banished from the new heaven and the new earth that were in the planning stage.

As a guarantee of the ultimate triumph of right, the *Book of Enoch* cited the fate of the rebel angels, called "sons of God" in Genesis 6:2, who "married as many as they chose" of the "daughters of men." This illicit series of unions bred a race of supermen called the Nephilim.

The people of Sodom and Gomorrah and their suburbs were like the rebel angels, says Jude, but with roles reversed. According to the story recorded in Genesis 18–19, Yahweh had sent two angels on a fact-finding mission. They received lodging at the home of Lot. The men of Sodom were far less hospitable and insisted that Lot hand the visitors over to their pleasure. Jude interpreted their deed as unnatural vice.

According to Genesis 6, rebel angels had taken the initiative in *successful* sexual union with human beings. At Sodom, human beings took the initiative in *attempted* illicit union with angels. With the force of an uncapped oil well blazing out of control, a bituminous explosion destroyed every Sodomite, with the exception of Lot's family.

STUDY QUESTION: Ordinarily we think of offbeat religious groups, political systems, and philosophies as hazards to the Christian faith. How does Jude clarify your thinking on this matter?

HAZARDOUS TO CHRISTIAN HEALTH

8 Nevertheless, these people are doing the same: in their delusions they not only defile their bodies and disregard authority, but abuse the glorious 9 angels as well. ·Not even the archangel Michael, when he was engaged in argument with the devil about the corpse of Moses, dared to denounce him in the language of abuse; all he said was, "Let 10 the Lord correct you." ·But these people abuse anything they do not understand; and the only things they do understand—just by nature like unreasoning animals—will turn out to be fatal to them.

11 May they get what they deserve, because they have followed Cain; they have rushed to make the same mistake as Balaam and for the same reward; they have rebelled just as Korah did—and share 12 the same fate. ·They are a dangerous obstacle to your community meals, coming for the food and quite shamelessly only looking after themselves. They are like clouds blown about by the winds and bringing no rain, or like barren trees which are then uprooted in the winter and so are twice 13 dead; ·like wild sea waves capped with shame as if with foam; or like shooting stars bound for 14 an eternity of black darkness. ·It was with them in mind that Enoch, the seventh patriarch from Adam, made his prophecy when he said, "I tell you, the Lord will come with his saints in their 15 tens of thousands, ·to pronounce judgment on all mankind and to sentence the wicked for all the wicked things they have done, and for all the de-

fiant things said against him by irreligious sin-
16 ners." ·They are mischief-makers, grumblers governed only by their own desires, with mouths full
of boastful talk, ready with flattery for other people when they see some advantage in it.

✠

Rebellion against divine authority and its invested
emissaries was the common denominator in the three
examples cited. With this as background Jude moves
decisively against those whom he considers threats to
the stability of the Christian community.

Several ancient authorities vouch for Jude's dependence on another popular noncanonical work, the *Assumption of Moses,* for the story about Michael. This
angel is mentioned also in Daniel 10:13, 21; 12:1.
And Revelation 12:7 states that he and the devil engaged in hostilities.

According to information that has come down to us,
the lost portion of the *Assumption of Moses* included a
scene of contention between Michael and the devil over
the possession of Moses' body. The devil affirmed that
as lord of the physical world he was entitled to claim
the body. Michael in turn attested God's ownership of
the entire world. The devil had to concede the point,
but indicted Moses for the slaying of an oppressive
Egyptian (cf. Ex 2:12). Yet in his disclaimer of the
devil's demand Michael observed the appropriate
amenities, says Jude. Such is not the case with the subversives who are undermining congregational life.

As verse 4 had emphatically stated, these rebels de-
spise the over-all authority of Jesus Christ. In imita-
tion, perhaps of St. Paul, they affirm their inde-
pendence from traditional instruction based on the
words of Jesus. They appear to claim superior under-

standing of theological matters and put on airs as privileged media for divine truth. But, affirms our author with trenchant sarcasm, their "revelations" are a wet-dream trip.

In matters about which they know nothing they pass themselves off as experts and deride their opposition. Other things they understand well—as do animals far lower on the zoological scale. And they manage to destroy themselves in the process. Born losers!

Then, with an economy of phrasing scarcely approached anywhere in polemical literature, Jude identifies them biographically with three of the worst criminals in Jewish tradition.

The first is a murderer, whose story is told in Genesis 4:1–24. In the course of tradition Cain became a symbol of deception and sensual self-interest.

The second is Balaam. Numbers 22–24 relates that the Moabites held him in high regard as a soothsayer. After an informational session with his jackass mount, Balaam sagely informed Balak, king of Moab, that Yahweh refused to desert Israel in favor of the Moabite cause.

Quite disconcerted, and like a gambler trying two out of three and then three out of seven, Balak tried to get a better reading by steering Balaam to two other mountain peaks, but the verdict remained the same. Israel would be the winner.

Unfortunately Balaam had a weakness for money. According to desert tradition he balanced the bad news for Balak with advice to place Moabite women at the disposal of the Israelite armies. Sex and idolatry are traditional bed companions, but idolatry and covenant do not mix, and Israel's census took a tumble of twenty-four thousand bodies (see Nb 25:9). As reward for his waffling Balaam was executed (Nb 31:8).

Like Balaam, opportunists in the Church appear to

have their eyes focused on God, but their minds are
fixed on temporal targets.

The final exhibit is **Korah.** Numbers 16–17 records
how he led a revolt of Levites against the authority of
Aaron's priesthood. An earthquake disposed of Korah,
his cronies, and their possessions. Jude's reference to
this subversive is the climactic clue to the real problem
in the congregations addressed: rebellion against traditional apostolic authority.

The total unreliability of the dissenters from apostolic teaching could scarcely find a more vivid description than that in verses 12–13. Jude's conglomerate of
metaphors concludes in verse 13 with an echo of verse
6 and anticipates the explicit reference to the *Book of
Enoch* in verses 14–15.

Enoch was the father of Methusaleh (see Gn
5:21–24). Enoch was such a good man that God personally "took him." In contrast to the subversives who
let their desires dictate their paths, Enoch "walked
with God."

Besides the *Book of Enoch,* cited in verses 14–15,
Jude again puts the *Assumption of Moses* under contribution, in verse 16. The combination makes it possible
for him to wind up his description of the rebels against
the background of two sets of three examples each,
sketched in verses 5–7 and 11. A charge of grumbling
on the part of the Israelites was a prominent prophetic
theme. The "saints in their tens of thousands" (verse
14) are the good angels. Like the rebellious angels
(verse 6) and all other disclaimers of divine authority,
the dissidents will receive their due punishment at the
hand of the Lord, who heads the *loyal* heavenly host.

Jude 17–25
BE VERY CAREFUL!

¹⁷ But remember, my dear friends, what the apostles of our Lord Jesus Christ told you to expect. ¹⁸ "At the end of time," they told you, "there are going to be people who sneer at religion and follow nothing but their own desires for wickedness." ·These unspiritual and selfish people are ¹⁹ nothing but mischief-makers.

The duties of love

²⁰ But you, my dear friends, must use your most holy faith as your foundation and build on that, ²¹ praying in the Holy Spirit; ·keep yourselves within the love of God and wait for the mercy of our ²² Lord Jesus Christ to give you eternal life. ·When there are some who have doubts, reassure them; ²³ when there are some to be saved from the fire, pull them out; but there are others to whom you must be kind with great caution, keeping your distance even from outside clothing which is contaminated by vice.

Doxology

²⁴ Glory be to him who can keep you from falling and bring you safe to his glorious presence, in- ²⁵ nocent and happy. ·To God, the only God, who saves us through Jesus Christ our Lord, be the glory, majesty, authority and power, which he had before time began, now and for ever. Amen.

✠

New converts especially may wonder about the gaps between the rhetoric and the performance of people who are in positions of leadership in Christendom. As to their presence, Jude reminds his addressees that the Lord's own apostles predicted their arrival. The fact is that nothing offers such opportunity for a con job as does Christianity. And there will always be those who are out to exploit its possibilities for self-advantage while boasting of their superior understanding (verse 19).

Far from invalidating the truth of the Christian message, their infiltration is a proof that Judgment Day is about to dawn (verses 17–18).

The best defense is an offense. Christianity is a cooperative enterprise, with each believer responsible for the other. The words "most holy faith" (verse 20) echo verse 3. With this terminology Jude reminds his addressees of the one Lord and Master who is pledged to them and elicits their commitment.

Argument is not always successful, and the admonition to keep one's distance (verse 23) is of a piece with the Pastor's counsel not to engage in disputes about words (2 Tm 2:14). Keep the door open and at times your mouth shut, is our writer's advice (verses 22–23).

The Great Day will come soon. Naturally the sincerely committed might be a little anxious. Will I make it? What if I fall into temptation?

To quiet their anxieties Jude writes about Judgment Day in a way that is surprising to many who think it should make one's hair stand on end. You will not be left to your own resources, he says. God will keep you from stumbling. Nor will you have to cringe in the divine presence. God will see to it that you are able to stand tall and be filled with joy that you, an outstanding citizen of the world, were privileged to please the Creator (verse 24).

In harmony with the general perspective of the Letter, Jude closes with a doxology that enunciates once more the theme of commitment to the Savior God who is committed to us in Jesus Christ (verse 25).

STUDY QUESTIONS: How can a Christian congregation best protect itself against exploitation by self-seeking leaders and yet maintain the spiritual qualities advocated by Jude? It has been said that Jude is not especially edifying. How do you react to such an evaluation?

SUGGESTED FURTHER READING

Most commentaries on these letters other than Hebrews include exposition of more than one letter. The letter A following a title indicates that the exposition is relatively fuller or more advanced than the comment in a title followed by the letter B.

Hebrews

Bretscher, P. G. *Cain, Come Home!* St. Louis: Clayton Publishing House, 1976. Not a commentary, but a brilliant study of the theme of reconciliation. (B)

Davies, J. H. *A Letter to Hebrews.* ("The Cambridge Bible Commentary"). Cambridge: Cambridge University Press, 1967. The commentaries in this series include the text of the New English Bible. (B)

Montefiore, H. *A Commentary on the Epistle to the Hebrews.* London: A. and C. Black, 1964. (A)

James

Mitton, C. L. *The Epistle of James.* Greenwood, S.C.: Attic Press, 1977. Based on the Revised Standard Version. (A)

Moffatt, J. *The General Epistles: James, Peter, and Judas.* ("The Moffatt New Testament Commentaries"). New York: Harper & Brothers, 1945. Based on the Moffatt translation of the Bible. (B)

Sidebottom, E. M. *James, Jude, and 2 Peter*. ("The New Century Bible"). Greenwood, S.C.: Attic Press, 1967. Based on the Revised Standard Version. (A)

Tasker, R. V. *The General Epistle of James*. ("The Tyndale New Testament Commentaries"). Grand Rapids, Mich.: Wm. B. Eerdmans Publishing Company, 1957. Based on the King James Version. (A)

Williams, R. R. *The Letters of John and James*. ("The Cambridge Bible Commentary"). Cambridge: Cambridge University Press, 1965. Based on the New English Bible. (B)

1 Peter

Best, E. *1 Peter*. ("The New Century Bible"). Greenwood, S.C.: Attic Press, 1971. (A)

Cranfield, C. E. *The First Epistle of Peter*. London: SCM Press, 1950. (B)

Kelly, J. *The Epistles of Peter and of Jude*. London: A. and C. Black, 1969. More detailed than Best and Stibbs. (A)

Moffatt, J. See under James.

Stibbs, A. M. *The First Epistle General of Peter*. ("The Tyndale Bible Commentaries"). Grand Rapids, Mich.: Wm. B. Eerdmans Publishing Company, 1959. (A)

2 Peter

Kelly, J. See under 1 Peter. (A)

Moffatt, J. See under James. (B)

Sidebottom, E. M. See under James. (A)

Wand, J. W. *The General Epistles of St. Peter and St. Jude*. ("Westminster Commentaries"). London:

Methuen and Company, 1934. Based on the Revised Version. (B)

1–3 John

Brown, R. E. *The Community of the Beloved Disciple.* New York: Paulist Press, 1979. (B)

Dodd, C. H. *The Johannine Epistles.* ("The Moffatt New Testament Commentaries"). New York: Harper & Brothers, 1946. (B)

Perkins, P. *The Johannine Epistles.* ("New Testament Message," 21). Wilmington, Delaware: Michael Glazier, 1979. (B)

Stott, J. R. *The Epistles of John.* ("The Tyndale New Testament Commentaries"). Grand Rapids, Mich.: Wm. B. Eerdmans Publishing Company, 1964. (A)

Williams, R. R. See under James. (B)

Jude

Moffatt, J. See under James. (B)

Sidebottom, E. M. See under James. (A)

Wand, J. W. See under 2 Peter. (B)

Briefer treatment is available in two notable one-volume commentaries:

The Jerome Biblical Commentary on the Bible, ed. R. E. Brown, J. A. Fitzmyer, and R. E. Murphy. Englewood Cliffs, N.J.: Prentice-Hall, 1968.

Peake's Commentary on the Bible, ed. M. Black and H. H. Rowley. London: Thomas Nelson & Sons, 1962. This commentary also contains an introductory article to "The Catholic Epistles," pp. 1020–21.

The series *Proclamation Commentaries* (Philadelphia: Fortress Press), offers a thematic digest of the contents of several of these letters under the titles *Hebrews, James, 1 and 2 Peter, Jude,* and *Revelation* (1977).

Still briefer aids to study include two series: *New Testament Reading Guide* (Collegeville, Minn.: The Liturgical Press), and *Herald Booklets* (Chicago: Franciscan Herald Press).

J. H. Elliott, *1 Peter: Estrangement and Community* (1979), is a part of the Herald series and offers a superb introduction to the social context of 1 Peter. (B)